THE
NAVAL ACADEMY CANDIDATE BOOK

HOW TO PREPARE
HOW TO GET IN
HOW TO SURVIVE

Third Edition

SUE ROSS

Silver Horn Books
Monument, CO

This book was produced with the full cooperation of the U.S. Navy and the U.S. Naval Academy. However, the author is solely responsible for its content.

Cover photo courtesy USNA Photography Branch

Copyright: © 2008 by Sue Ross (Third Edition); second printing 2009
            1997 by William L. Smallwood (Second Edition)

All rights reserved. No part of this book may be reproduced or transmitted in any form or by any means without permission of the publisher, except in the case of brief quotations embodied in critical articles and reviews. For information contact Silver Horn Books, c/o Sierra Consulting, 20030 Silver Horn Ln., Monument, CO 80132.

Although the author and publisher have exhaustively researched all sources to ensure the accuracy and completeness of the information contained in this book, we assume no responsibility for errors, inaccuracies, omissions, or any inconsistency herein. Any slights of people or organizations are unintentional.

ISBN 978-0-9797943-1-5

Printed and bound in the United States of America

6/23

TABLE OF CONTENTS

Introduction

Acknowledgements

THE NAVAL ACADEMY OFFICIAL MISSION

To develop midshipmen
morally, mentally and
physically and to imbue
them with the highest ideals
of duty, honor and loyalty
in order to provide graduates
who are dedicated to a
career of naval service and
have potential for future
development in mind and
character to assume the
highest responsibilities
of command, citizenship
and government.

A WORD FROM THE AUTHOR

Do you think you might want to go to the United States Naval Academy?

Then visit their web site and study it. The admissions web address is www.usna.edu/admissions, and you can find additional information about the Naval Academy at www.usna.edu. You will learn the history of the institution, the kinds of courses you can take, and the specifications of the physical and medical examinations that you must pass. You will find out if and when you are eligible to apply, and learn in great detail about the many steps in the lengthy admissions process.

This book has very little of the above material. Instead, this book will give you a clear picture of what you are getting into, based on the advice and experience of hundreds of midshipmen, graduates, faculty, and staff officers. This is a "how to" book.

This book will tell you how to prepare for the Academy.

One chapter, which is probably the most important one in the book, tells you how to prepare mentally. This chapter will help you examine your motives for attending the Academy, motives that have a big influence on your chances for success. Other chapters tell you how to prepare academically, physically and in other important ways.

This book will tell you how to get into the Academy.

One chapter describes all the procedures, including how and when to get started as well as how to become more competitive. Another chapter describes how to get a congressional nomination and some of the pitfalls of that process. Other chapters give you guidelines on how to conduct yourself during interviews, and how you might be able to get into the Academy by alternate routes if you are now unqualified or have failed to get in by the regular process.

This book will also tell you how to survive when you get to the Academy.

In one chapter you learn about the first year, the "plebe year," which from a physical and psychological standpoint is by far the hardest. In other chapters the midshipmen tell you what you must do to succeed militarily, academically, and physically; special advice is given to intercollegiate athletes, women and others who will be in the minority at the Academy. Later, if you decide to go and receive an appointment, I suggest you read and reread these chapters.

The final chapter is for parents. Parents from around the United States who have had sons and daughters at the Academy share some of the hard lessons they learned. Midshipmen also reveal what they want and need for support from home.

Beyond giving you "how-to" advice, this book gives you a close-up look at the challenges and opportunities that only the Naval Academy provides, so that you can determine whether it is the right place for you. You are advised to read through this book if you are just thinking about going to the Naval Academy. If I have succeeded, by the time you are done you will either 1) Realize that your hopes and dreams are best pursued at a more traditional college or university, or 2) Be more determined than ever to become a midshipman.

If the latter is your choice, then STUDY this book. You will be one of many smart and talented young men and women competing for a limited number of openings. The application process itself is difficult … by design.

Besides meeting all the qualifications and having good information and advice, you need one other thing, something that no one else can give you: You need desire. You need desire that keeps you up at night and focuses your energy and drives you over all the hurdles that may be thrown in front of you. That desire will get you into the Naval Academy, and that desire will get you through the Naval Academy. If you are easily discouraged or don't feel that burning desire, get a catalog from State U. and save yourself lots of headaches.

A final word: Thousands upon thousands of young men and women have made it into the Naval Academy before you, and managed to graduate. Some served in the Navy or Marine Corps for 35 years, becoming admirals or generals and leading thousands of other men and women. Some served for the minimum five years and then began a career in the civilian world. Either way, practically all of them will tell you that attending the Naval Academy was one of the greatest experiences of their life—that it made them into something they would never have become without that experience.

If you really want to push yourself to your limit every single day, get a great education, then serve your country and see the world … go for it!

SCR

THE INSTITUTION

ONE
The Academic Institution

The United States Naval Academy sits on 338 acres located at the mouth of the Severn River on the Chesapeake Bay, surrounded by the growing city of Annapolis, Maryland.

The Naval Academy opened in 1845, with a faculty of seven. Many of the buildings now in use, including the dormitory known as Bancroft Hall, were built in the late 1800s or early 1900s. The architecture is reminiscent of pre-World War I France. A memorial honors John Paul Jones, the father of the American Navy. While the students (called midshipmen, or "mids" for short) are busy with the high-tech curriculum and preparing to serve in the 21st century, they are all keenly aware of their link to a proud tradition that dates back some 230 years.

The first midshipmen completed a five-year program including two years at sea in order to become naval officers. Today, the Naval Academy is a four-year college that grants Bachelor of Science degrees and officer commissions to its graduates. The students are still called midshipmen, and sea duty is still required before they graduate—mids must complete short cruises during the summer.

Despite the strong link to the past, the Naval Academy's curriculum places heavy emphasis on science and technology. The Navy prides itself on

Aerial view of the Naval Academy and Annapolis. The large building in the center is Bancroft Hall. ANN ARUNDEL COUNTY VISITORS BUREAU

3

employing the best of modern technology on its ships, aircraft, and submarines. From nuclear-powered aircraft carriers to cruise missiles and communications networks, the Navy requires its officers to be comfortable with the most sophisticated technology.

The Naval Academy is accredited by the Middle States Association. Also, six engineering majors, computer science, and chemistry are accredited by their respective professional accreditation organizations.

Accreditation is really just a passing grade. Just how good is the academic program at the Naval Academy? A few other indicators will tell you. One measure is how the graduates do on the Fundamentals of Engineering Examination—a test engineers take to get licensed. Of Naval Academy graduates who take the test, 85 percent pass on the first try. Graduates of other engineering colleges average about 70 percent.

Naval Academy graduates also win more than their share of awards for graduate studies, including the prestigious Rhodes and Marshall Scholarships, as well as Guggenheim and National Science Foundation Fellowships.

> *The* **Princeton Review**
> *ranked the Naval Academy*
> *third in the nation for "most*
> *accessible professors."*

Other indicators will tell you that the Naval Academy is one of the nation's best colleges. The U.S. Naval Academy was ranked as the country's 20th best liberal arts college by *US News*, and third in undergraduate engineering programs. The *Princeton Review* ranked the Naval Academy third in the nation for "most accessible professors."

This last achievement, highly accessible professors, provides a clue as to what makes the Naval Academy's program so unique and highly respected. Much of the credit is due the faculty. It is a teaching faculty. The professors do not have the research obligations they do in most other top institutions. Naval Academy professors' main job is to teach, not to publish research papers in their field of expertise.

Another strength of the Naval Academy faculty is its tradition for giving extra instruction, or "EI." Each professor sets aside certain hours each day that are used by the midshipmen for EI. Many even encourage their students to call them at home after hours.

Mids will take an average of 18 hours each semester, about 20 percent more than their friends at civilian schools. Why does the Academy place such a premium on academics? It is a military school after all.

One Academy official explained their high standards this way: "What you have to remember is that we have to hire all our graduates. Other four-year institutions can graduate theirs, then turn them loose and forget about them. When our graduates leave here and take their jobs in the Navy [or Marine Corps], they have to perform well, often under adverse

Professors at the Naval Academy are dedicated to teaching.   USNA Photo Lab

circumstances. Obviously, we do not want to hear anything bad about our graduates, so we put extra effort into seeing that we do our job right."

The Naval Academy is clearly a fine college, especially for those who want to study science and technology. But there is much more to the Naval Academy.

It is first and foremost a very tough military institution with the mission to develop the highest quality officers to lead in the Navy and Marine Corps. How they go about doing that is the focus of the next chapter.

TWO
The Military Institution

You will certainly get a first rate education at the Naval Academy, but you can get a great education at many excellent colleges or universities.

You get a whole lot more at the Naval Academy. Besides a Bachelor of Science degree, you also get four years of intense leadership training, and experiences you cannot match anywhere else. When you graduate, you receive a commission as an officer in the Navy or Marine Corps, and a guaranteed job.

If you are thinking about applying for the Naval Academy, it is very important that you understand what the Navy expects of its officers.

Almost without exception, midshipmen become different people from who they were in high school, usually within the first few weeks. They become so different, if fact, that their parents and friends often look at them and wonder what happened to the young man or woman they used to know.

The Navy wants officers who are smart and adaptable. They want them physically strong, and of good moral character. Most important, they want good leaders who are willing to serve their country in time of war.

They want the kind of leaders who thrive on new and difficult challenges. They want leaders who can withstand the incredible pressures of warfare—the kind who can remain cool and effective when surrounded by chaos or under fire.

Finally, they want leaders who understand and believe strongly in the American concept of government and freedom. They must be willing to go to war and, if necessary, die in the performance of such duty.

What all of the above means for the midshipman is quite simple. "College life" at the Naval Academy is not anything like it is at Home State University.

At the Naval Academy, the students are focused on what they will be asked to do after they graduate. While they do not welcome war, or want to go into harm's way, they would never be satisfied to sit back and let someone else do it for them. Every day of their four years at Annapolis is shaped by that understanding.

INTO THE PRESSURE COOKER: PLEBE SUMMER

The Naval Academy experience begins on a steamy summer day in July called Induction Day, or "I-Day." The new midshipmen, known as "plebes," check in, get their uniforms and equipment and learn how to salute. They say goodbye to most of their hair and the carefree life they left behind.[1] The first day ends in a swearing in ceremony and a final goodbye to Mom and Dad.

---

1. Men get the traditional head shaving, a practical haircut for the summer heat and humidity. Women must have their hair above their collar.

From the beginning of Plebe Summer, you will know that you are not attending an ordinary college. USNA PHOTO LAB

Then the heat turns up. The upperclassmen, called detailers, will not be your friends, but they will make sure you learn what you need to know, and push yourself to your limits.

Plebe Summer lasts about six weeks. During this period, every minute of your day is controlled by the detailers. You will be pushed to your limits—limits of stress endurance, physical stamina, patience, tolerance, commitment, mental concentration and character. You will learn discipline, and perseverence. You will also learn pride, confidence, and teamwork.

When you are not running or doing physical training, you will learn about the Navy—its history, traditions, and customs. You will learn basic lessons of seamanship and sailing. You will also start to adjust to some of the realities of the next four years: There will always be more to do than you can fit into a 24 hour day, and everything you do will be evaluated and critiqued.

Some midshipmen say that Plebe Summer is the most difficult part of their four years at the Naval Academy. It is definitely a huge adjustment period, especially for those who have no experience with military life.

While many plebes expect that once Plebe Summer is over life will be easier, once the academic year starts they often find themselves longing for the simple life of Plebe Summer.

FULL STEAM AHEAD: THE DEMANDS OF PLEBE YEAR

After Plebe Summer is over, you will begin a full load of demanding academic courses. The entire brigade will have returned, and the upper three classes will all share in the task of further indoctrinating the plebes. Also, plebes will begin their professional military training in "pro classes."

Sound like a lot to manage? That is not all. All midshipmen are required to participate in competitive sports, either intercollegiate or intramural. Sports foster a competitive spirit and winning mindset, and establish a habit of fitness the Navy expects of its Sailors. Midshipmen participate in a wide variety of sports, including tradition team sports and individual sports.

Sailing is one of the most important non-traditional sports at the Academy. Throughout their four years, midshipmen learn on the Academy's fleet of 198 craft, one of the largest fleets of sailing craft in the world.

Everything you do will be evaluated and critiqued.   USNA Photo Lab

During Plebe Summer, every minute was scheduled for you. You were told exactly what to do and when to do it. Once the academic year begins, you have to figure out on your own how to juggle all the competing demands.

The plebe year is stressful, exhausting, and frustrating. During darker moments, many plebes think about their friends relaxing and partying at a college closer to home. They find themselves wondering why the Naval Academy has to be so difficult. There is one simple and very important reason. Remember, the Naval Academy is designed to produce quality naval officers.

What is a naval officer? The term applies to officers in two of the military services: the Navy and the Marine Corps. Each year, seniors elect to serve in either the Navy or Marine Corps. In recent years, more midshipmen request to serve in the Marine Corps than there are slots available.

In addition to choosing which branch of service to join, seniors choose a career field. They may elect to serve in the surface Navy, which includes ships ranging from small frigates to carriers. They may elect to serve in submarines or aviation. Graduates who enter the Marine Corps may select to be part of the ground forces or Marine aviation.

What determines what assignment a graduate will get? Academic grades matter, as does military performance during the four years at the Academy. Midshipmen are also rated on athletic performance, as well as their performance during summer programs.

The haircut on Induction Day symbolizes the end of your old, carefree life.   USNA Photo Lab

As a general rule, most midshipmen get their first or second choice of assignment. However, those with the highest class standings get to pick their assignments first.

All graduates are expected to serve for at least five years. That is the commitment they make when they begin their third year. If midshipmen resign from the Academy after the beginning of their third year, they are obligated to serve in the enlisted force to repay the cost of their education.

By the time they reach the commitment point, midshipmen have had plenty of time to work through that decision. In fact, many midshipmen who originally came to the Naval Academy unsure of their intentions make that commitment with great assurance. They have formed a bond with their fellow midshipmen, and a sense of duty to the Navy. The question "Should I stay?" turns into "How long will my naval career be?"

CAN I MAKE IT AT THE NAVAL ACADEMY?

By the end of the first year, plebes have proven to themselves and the upperclassmen that they have the potential to be good officers. They have examined their motives for being at the Academy, and come to terms with their own strengths and weaknesses. They have thought hard about what it means to be a leader. The plebe year put them to the test and in the process made them stronger.

During Plebe Summer, you will learn the fundmentals of sailing. USNA Photo Lab

If you are a potential candidate, but worried about the rigors of military training, keep two things in mind.

First, keep in mind that the Naval Academy has one of the highest survival rates of any college in the United States. About 80 percent of all those who enter the Academy survive all four years and graduate. That number is far above the national average for all colleges.

Why is the graduation rate so high? One of the reasons is the rigorous application process. Only about one in ten potential candidates meets all the requirements, finishes the entire process, and receives and accepts an appointment. If you are one of those appointees, then you have already proven that you have what it takes to succeed at the Naval Academy. As long as you have the desire and the determination.

Second, do not reject the idea of being a candidate until you have read what the midshipmen themselves say about surviving. Their advice can help you decide if you can make it, too.

With the end of the plebe year, the worst is over, but there are still three rigorous years ahead. Is it worth it? The next chapter provides an answer to this question from the perspective of some graduates who have succeeded in a variety of military and civilian career fields.

THREE:
Graduates Speak: What The Academy Experience Did For Me

Rear Admiral (retired) Don Boecker, Class of 1960

Admiral Boecker enlisted in the Naval Reserve, then went to prep school for a year before attending the Academy where he played four years of varsity football and golf. An aviation buff since he was a boy, he went to flight training after graduation. His first deployment was on the USS Enterprise, *which was put on alert for the Cuban Missile Crisis in 1963. He deployed to Vietnam with the first A-6 Intruder squadron, flying 69 combat missions from the carrier* Independence. *On one mission, a bomb exploded as it was released and he and his bombardier ejected, evaded the enemy, and were rescued 18 hours later by a heroic helicopter crew while under heavy enemy fire. After Vietnam he went to Test Pilot School and held several command positions including commander of the* USS Concord *and commander of the Naval Air Test Center. He retired as Vice Commander, Naval Air Systems Command.*

In preparing for this interview I didn't have to think very long to make a list of the things that the Naval Academy did for me. There were some black days when I was going there, particularly that first year, but looking

Don Boecker (second from right) is being congratulated after his rescue from a rice paddy in Laos while Don Eaton, his bombardier/navigator (left) looks on.   DON BOECKER

11

back with my current perspective, they were truly golden years and it is real easy to tell you why.

First is the discipline. It was tough at first, and I will admit that it was very hard dealing with it. But the discipline that was imposed upon me as a plebe gave me the foundation for establishing my own self-discipline as I went through the next three years. And later, when I started flying airplanes, the rules and regulations made sense to me, and allowed me to fly aggressively but safely, because I respected the limitations and the rationale behind the regulations—and that has kept me alive while flying over 90 different models of Navy and Marine aircraft.

Second is the physical conditioning. I cannot say enough about the value of daily exercise, which I started during Plebe Summer and have continued to this day. I learned that exercise helps a person stay sharp both mentally and physically. It was a good lesson and it has helped me throughout my career.

Third is competitiveness. The Academy requires every midshipman to participate in some kind of sport, and that's an excellent requirement. The idea of teamwork has to be instilled in young people who will become our officers because they in turn will have to instill that in the young men and women we have today on our ships. That's the only way we can empower and use the talents of young people; they have to learn that they can always do something better as a team rather than as individuals.

The idea of teamwork has to be instilled in young people who will become our officers...

My friend and bombardier/navigator, Rear Admiral Don Eaton, USN (retired), and I have recently celebrated the 19th anniversary of our 15 July 1965 rescue from an enemy-ridden rice paddy in the remote hill country of Laos, where we were downed on a classified bombing mission. Neither of us could have lived without our military training that had given us immense self-discipline and great physical conditioning. I was 27 years old, and without the spirit of competitiveness instilled in me by the rigors of Academy life, I could not have fought through that confrontation with the enemy with self-confidence and with the spirit of teamwork Don and I used to get us through.

Fourth is time management. One cannot survive at the Naval Academy with the strong academic load, professional training, and daily athletic practice without learning to manage time. It is tough, really tough, at first when there is never enough time to do everything. But this teaches one to carefully plan each day to make sure every time slot is accounted for. Also, it teaches one to avoid the kinds of things that can divert you and wreck plans. Later, when I was pressed for time and under pressure, I could fall back on this training. Now after 34 years in many kinds of jobs, I can really appreciate what that training did for me.

The fifth thing I learned is most important, although it started with the lessons taught by my own family as I was growing up. I learned to get along with people. I learned to treat people with dignity, and like I would like to be treated. That lesson carried over in every one of my commands. There are many characteristics of a good leader, but I don't know of a single one who is really great who does not have this talent. I cannot emphasize this enough. To motivate people, you have to treat them with dignity. When I was at the Academy, there was great emphasis placed on the responsibility of an officer to be a gentleman and a moral leader. They taught us it is not enough to be bright or well-trained. They stressed that a good officer must strive to be an exemplary human being.

How would I be different if I had not gone to the Academy? I always liked math and science, and I would probably have gone on to become an engineer in some company. But I would be a different person, and my outlook on life would probably be totally different. In the Navy I have had the opportunity to meet many thousands of people. I have seen hundreds of countries and know about the values and cultures of their people. As an engineer in some company, I don't think I would be nearly as proud of being an American as I am now. My vision of the world helps me put America in perspective. My experiences in the Navy have helped me realize what a truly great country we have.

Captain (retired) Mike McGrath, Class of 1962

Captain McGrath was a varsity wrestler for Navy, qualifying for national championships twice. After graduation he became an A-4 pilot, and was shot down on his 179th combat mission over North Vietnam. He was a POW for almost six years in the notorious prison known as the "Hanoi Hilton." After being repatriated in 1973, he served as a squadron commander, a department head at the Naval Academy, and an attaché in Ecuador. After retiring, he flew for United Airlines and also served as president of a Vietnam POW organization. He also authored and illustrated the book Prisoner of War: Six Years in Hanoi.

I grew up in Delta, Colorado, a small town with no ROTC program and no one who knew much about the military. My senior year in high school, I was invited to a luncheon to see a midshipman home on leave give a presentation about the Naval Academy, and I was fascinated. The fire was lit.

I was a good student, I was captain of the wrestling team, and I participated in a lot of extracurricular activities. My test scores weren't good enough the first year, so my congressman encouraged me to try again next year. I went to the University of Colorado on a one-year wrestling

Then-Ensign McGrath in 1963, when he was in flight training. MIKE MCGRATH

scholarship, then retook my tests and got appointments to both the Naval Academy and the Air Force Academy, which was just being built.

Plebe Summer was the shock of my life. I was totally unprepared—I didn't even know what a reef point was.[1] I excelled in the physical aspects, but I didn't memorize my plebe rates as well as I should. That put me in for a rough six months. It can be tough when an upperclassman asks you a question in the morning you don't know the answer to, and says, "Find out by the noon meal." When would I do that? I have classes all morning. So he asks you again at noon meal and you still don't know, so as punishment he piles on more work to have done by dinner.

You will get torn down as a plebe; you're about the lowest human being on the earth, but you survive and you're proud to get through it. You become a survivor. In my company of 45 plebes, 22 resigned by Christmas—it was a tough company. Once when I was having a bad day I called home to complain, and my mom told me, "Get back to work; don't come crying home." She was right.

I think sports really helped me at the Naval Academy. Athletes are used to being beat up. My freshman year in high school, I got pinned every match, but by junior year I was going for the championship. As athletes we know how to start at the bottom, get up each day with bruises and aches and pains, and go back out there for more. You have to have staying power to fight through defeat.

The first time I stepped in an airplane was an indoctrination flight my plebe year, in an N3N biplane, wearing goggles and a leather helmet. I set my goal right then to finish high enough in my class to be an aviator. That's another lesson you learn at the Naval Academy—setting and reaching goals. Once you graduate, you know how to reach any goal. Graduating is just the first step.

---

1. *Reef Points* is the book of plebe knowledge that every midshipman must memorize. The name reef point refers to a length of cord used to secure excess fabric on a sail.

After four years there, you're a different person. You're a leader with confidence, you're adventurous, and you can hold your own for the rest of your life. Sportsmanship, courage, competitiveness, setting goals—you learn all those things.

By far the most important thing I learned at the Naval Academy was how to survive. When I was taken prisoner on June 30th, 1967, I had a broken arm, a dislocated shoulder, and a fractured spine. They tortured me for days at a time, and dislocated my elbow and my other shoulder. I received no medical attention, and I had infections all over my body. Part of me wished I could die.

But I had learned during my plebe year that I could survive anything. That was the most valuable thing I learned. Going up against tough people in a tough sport helped. Surviving all the engineering courses helped too! Through all the torture as a POW, the only truthful answer I ever gave the enemy was the names of my wife and children, in case I got any letters (which I did three years after I was captured). The rest of the time I made things up, because if you stopped talking the pain started again. Once, I told them we had a swimming pool and tennis courts on the aircraft carrier.

My advice to candidates is to put away childish things and make mature decisions. Start early and don't waste time. Develop good study habits, get straight A's, prepare for your SATs, and be a leader in extracurricular activities. You have to be serious about where you're going or you won't be competitive. No one will hand it to you. You really have to grow up faster than the other kids.

Plebe year, be tougher than the other guys. There's no easy way to get through it. You will get put down, yelled at, and insulted. You have to get back up and keep going. I told my son [Commander Rick McGrath graduated from the Naval Academy in 1987]: "You got straight A's in High School, but so did everyone else. You're going to get some B's or C's and it will knock the wind out of you. You're not perfect anymore; you're a normal, mortal human being." You have to be ready for that, and not become defeated.

I'm so proud of the Academy's reputation, my classmates who graduated with me, our sports teams. The Naval Academy prepares you for life, and the lessons you learn there will pay off all your life. Set your goals, and go for them.

Admiral Mike Mullen, Class of 1968

Admiral Mullen was raised in North Hollywood, California, with both parents working in the movie industry. He was a recruited basketball player out of high school, and elected the Naval Academy "because I knew I needed the discipline." By Christmas his first year he was on the borderline of failure, but persisted and went on to graduate, selecting surface warfare as a career. His first assignment was on a destroyer which deployed in

Vietnamese waters during the war. While still a lieutenant, he commanded his first ship, a gasoline tanker. He returned to the Naval Academy for a three-year tour (two as a company officer) before returning to sea duty. He has commanded Cruiser/Destroyer Battle Group Two, the George Washington Battle Group, the U.S. 2nd Fleet, NATO Joint Force Command Naples and U.S. Naval Forces Europe. He served as the Chief of Naval Operations before becoming the Chairman of the Joint Chiefs of Staff, the highest ranking military officer in the U.S.

As Chairman of the Joint Chiefs of Staff, Admiral Mullen serves as principal military advisor to the President and Secretary of Defense.
DEPARTMENT OF DEFENSE

I'll start out with a little story that will help explain the main effect the Academy had on me. I was a young lieutenant, 26 years old, when I took command of the *USS Noxubee*, a small gasoline tanker with a crew of about 100 men. In that tour we had to return to the United States from a deployment in the Mediterranean. As we got into the Atlantic, this huge storm front extended from Nova Scotia to South America and, all alone in the Atlantic, we hit 40-foot seas and we were stuck in that storm for 96 hours—four days—around the clock.

We were in the infamous Bermuda Triangle at the time. The young boots from Iowa and Nebraska and Idaho—kids on their first cruise who had never dreamed of anything like we were experiencing—started coming to me with these books about the mysterious sinkings in that Triangle. But throughout those 96 hours, when I probably got a total of four hours sleep, and when the ship was rising, then slamming down so hard that it seemed like it would break, and when the waves were 15 feet above my eye level from my position in the bridge, and when one wrong move would have caused the ship to capsize and kill us all, it never entered my mind that we might not survive. I was totally strong and confident the whole time, and my point in saying all this is because the Naval Academy gave me a massive package that let me do all that with supreme confidence.

I remember walking on the *USS Collett*, a destroyer, for my first assignment. I wasn't sure the Navy was for me, or that I would even like being on a ship. But, from the minute I walked on that deck, a feeling came over me and I knew that I was in the right place. That, too, is what the Naval Academy did for me.

How did the Academy do that? It was a very simple but very hard lesson. From that first day, when the temperature was 95 degrees and the humidity was 90 percent, I had to learn discipline and perseverance. I had to learn to overcome adversity. And, later, when this jerk decided he was going to run me out of the Academy, whatever raw leadership ability I had came out. I said to myself that I was not going to let someone like that beat me—that I am going to persevere and turn what he thinks is going to be a big loss into a big win. And I did. I survived, and that jerk really did me a favor because the experience gave me confidence. Of course, throughout the other three years, I went on to learn more about leadership, and when I hit the deck of that first destroyer, I was ready. I was confident. I was ready for the excitement and the challenges that I knew we would face on a day-by-day basis.

So the Naval Academy took the raw material I had for leadership and gave me the knowledge, the strength, and the confidence to become a good leader—one who is never better than when things are at their absolute worst.

It taught me humility, which is a very important trait for a leader to have

There are some other things the Academy did for me that I should also mention. I learned the importance of teamwork, and learned to place team goals ahead of personal goals. It taught me humility, which is a very important trait for a leader to have. Also, I thrived in an environment based upon honesty and integrity. I didn't see much of that in my high school; cheating was common and an everyday occurrence. I welcomed the atmosphere at the Academy where one learned to trust your classmates.

Speaking of classmates, I should mention the strong bonds of friendship that are established at the Academy. When I went back for a high school reunion after twenty years, I felt like a stranger to most of my classmates. We had little in common. But when I went to my 20-year Academy reunion, we picked up on conversations with each other just as though we had seen each other just yesterday. The feeling was totally different, and having so many close friends is a bonus the Academy gives its graduates.

Finally, I should mention something personal. I have always had a social conscience and I like the idea of serving others. Consequently, it was a bit of a shock for me when I went to Harvard with all these hot runners—young men and women executives on the fast track. Don't get me wrong; they were good guys and gals—very bright and capable. But their narrowness of experience and goals just flabbergasted me. But that is the business world. We studied a whole bunch of companies and there were only two or three that I would even consider if I were looking for a job. Service to society is more important to me, and more satisfying. In fact, when the day comes for me to leave the Navy, I want to give service to somebody. I'm sure that the Academy, along with my career experiences, helped develop that attitude.

Bob Walters credits the Naval Academy for his success as a CEO.   BOB WALTERS

Bob Walters, Class of 1979

Bob Walters grew up in a suburb of Pittsburgh. He graduated 4th in the Class of '79, then went to graduate school at Princeton on a Guggenheim Fellowship. He logged over 1,800 hours flying Marine F/A-18s until he was medically retired from the Marine Corps. He has been the vice president or general manager for six Silicon Valley startup software companies and chief executive officer for two. He is now CEO of a security software company. He has also written articles on the leadership lessons he learned at the Naval Academy.

I grew up in a classic Midwestern steel town during the Apollo [space program] era, and my dream was to become an astronaut. I figured the way to become astronaut was to become a military pilot, preferably a fighter pilot.

At the time, I had long hair and was a do-my-own-thing kind of guy, so I wanted to do the military thing the easiest way I could. My plan was to go to Carnegie Mellon or Cornell, and join ROTC because we didn't have money to pay for college.

Then I got a letter from the commandant of midshipmen my junior year in high school. They wanted me to talk to the crew coach, and invited me to visit for a weekend.

So I went to Annapolis and fell in love with it. I loved the facilities, the history and traditions, the whole man concept. I was impressed by the fact that the instructors were there to teach me and not do research, so I thought it would be a great place to learn—I'm a scholar and that appealed to me.

So I reported with the Class of '79, and it was a shock. I had been planning for the worst mentally, expecting a pretty heavy duty saga. But it was a shock. All through Plebe Summer, I just had a bit of a bunker mentality—I just kept my head down and did it. It never crossed my mind to quit. I wasn't sure how much pain it would entail, but I was going to do it.

Learning rates [plebe knowledge] was the worst thing. I hated the rote memorization, and I'm not really good at it. I hated rates, and I hated marching. Marching was the worst, even when I was the regimental commander out in front. I thought we did way too much of it. Later, when I became a Marine, I loved going to 8th and I, but we were far from that level.[2]

When the academic year started, I came out of the bunker mentality. Now I was on my turf because I'm an academic guy. As soon as I made superintendent's list, things changed. I felt proud about it.[3] I felt like I got upperclassmen's respect, though they didn't show it overtly.

I quickly decided I was going to graduate first in my class. That became my overarching goal, and that goal governed my study habits. I majored in systems engineering. Starting my youngster [sophomore] year, I decided to overload to get more 4.0 credits to offset any B's I might get.

I was still focused on being an astronaut, but knew I wouldn't graduate and become an astronaut right away. I made a very provocative selection given my class ranking—going into the Marine Corps wasn't a popular choice then. Admiral Rickover thought I was crazy.[4] But I had my aviation slot locked in.

I figured if I was going to war, I wanted to do it with the toughest warfighters.

Why did I choose the Marines? Two reasons. I figured if I was going to war, I wanted to do it with the toughest warfighters. There was another, more pragmatic reason: While I definitely didn't mind flying off a carrier occasionally, Navy guys spent less time dropping bombs and [practicing] air to air [combat maneuvers]. Marine aviators didn't build our whole lives around the carrier like the Navy did.

I flew F/A-18s until I was medically retired in 1988. That ended the pilot and astronaut dream. After that, I spent almost a decade in the Washington, D.C. area as a consultant doing interesting projects for the Pentagon in areas like air combat simulation and artificial intelligence. I wanted to get into selling products, so I moved to Silicon Valley.

---

2. The Marines from the Marine Corps Barracks perform a moving and impressive Evening Parade ceremony in Washington D.C. at 8th and I Streets on Friday evenings in the summer.

3. The superintendent's list recognizes those midshipmen who meet strict criteria for academic grades, military performance, and physical fitness. Those mids who make the list get extra privileges and wear a gold start on their uniform.

4. Admiral Hyman Rickover is considered the Father of the Nuclear Navy. He was known not only for his vision, but also for his gruff, draconian leadership style. Bob Walters was far from the first to be thrown out of the Admiral's office.

My path would have been very different if I hadn't gone to the Naval Academy. I would fail at this job if I didn't understand the power of teams. In order to lead, you have to know how to follow, and how to be a team-member. That's a core cultural lesson that the plebe year is trying to teach: It ain't all about you. The Academy, the Navy, the world ain't all about you, and your gratification. You have to start thinking beyond yourself. You have to think about your team.

I remember talking to former Medal of Honor recipient and POW Admiral James Stockdale when I was a midshipman. We asked him how he got through it, and did all the heroic things he did. This was his response: "I just couldn't let the other boys down. It was unthinkable. They needed me. We needed each other. The other Medal winners that I've asked said similar things…we did it for our team." If you learn the power of team, and the power of trust in teams…wow, that's a big lesson! It absolutely makes me a better CEO.

My advice to anyone considering applying is to take a good look at Annapolis. I didn't want to go when I got that invitation, then things totally changed for me. I have no idea what it is or isn't going to do for you; it's a personal decision. And let me tell you that it isn't free; you have to give up a lot.

My survival advice? Don't overthink things. Part of what plebe year is about is changing you, and if you're trying to outsmart the changers, you thwart the whole process and make it harder for yourself. You have to trust that they're doing this for a reason, and it will end…even if that trust is intellectually unfounded. Plebe Summer is constructed as a change agent, and you can't evaluate life-changing things while you're in the middle of it. After you've had a good taste of the academic year, maybe at Thanksgiving, take a look at things if you still have serious doubts. You just don't know what you're evaluating if you do that in the heat of battle. In my experience, midshipmen get fouled up when they start to doubt. That leads to attitude problems that lead to performance problems.

The Naval Academy changed my life, no question. I was unstructured, long haired, undisciplined, and most things came easy for me…and that was good enough. At Navy, I learned how to be driven. Until you've been driven you don't know how to drive.

Captain (retired) Wendy Lawrence, class of 1981

Prior to becoming an astronaut, Captain Lawrence served as an H-46 "Sea Knight" helicopter pilot—one of the first of three women to make a long deployment supporting a carrier battle group. After that tour, she was sent to the Massachusetts Institute of Technology to obtain a Master's Degree in Ocean Engineering, then back to flight operations, flying an H-2 helicopter doing oceanographic research. She then went to the Naval Academy to teach physics and coach women's crew before being accepted for astronaut training. She has logged 1,225 hours in space on four different space shuttle missions. Captain Lawrence retired from NASA in 2006 and now works for a commercial space company.

The best thing about the Academy is what it teaches you about yourself. The environment there encourages you to be the best that you can be, and it gives you the opportunities to do that. You really learn about yourself through failure, and during your plebe year the system makes sure that you experience failure. Then, after you have failed, you are faced with a choice. Do you pick yourself up

Astronaut Wendy Lawrence has logged over 1,225 hours in space.   NASA

and move on, or do you stay flat on your back, defeated? From this, if you persevere, you become dedicated and determined, and, because of the demands of the system, you become committed to excellence.

Plebe year is tough. Every day there is a new challenge. You are always tired because you never get enough sleep. The stress and the pressure are always there and the easiest thing is to give up, especially after you think you have tried as hard as you can. But the great strength of the Academy is the support that comes from your classmates, the faculty and the officers who are stationed there. So, with this support, you find the strength and continue, and, after that, you begin to feel good about yourself. You then look inside yourself and you see a new person, a better person; you have learned that there is more inside yourself that you ever imagined.

Another thing I carried away from the Academy was an attitude toward failure. I am not afraid of challenges. I am not thinking about failure. The attitude I developed was to always do your best, then you never have to hang your head if you fail.

It is also important to point out some of the enjoyable things about the Academy experience. For me, the close personal relationships I developed are the most memorable. There is a very strong bond that you develop between your classmates. Later, you realize that this bond is going to last throughout your lifetime. In addition, if you are on an athletic team, the rowing team for example, you perform physically demanding work every day, in the rain and in the cold, and the adversity you share causes you to develop a very, very strong bond with your teammates.

But the Academy is not for everybody. I stress this when I speak to high school students. You are not in control of your life when you are there. It's not like a civilian school where you can go into town when you wish, and where the choice of studying is your own. You have a schedule laid out for you, you are told which uniform you have to wear, and you have to perform when you don't feel like it.

But that's the way it is when you're in the fleet. You are not in control. You go where they send you. And, if you're on flight operations 24 hours a day and don't feel like flying, that's too bad. You have a job to do and you have to do it.

Personally, I never found the regimentation a problem. I like organization and structure; I'm comfortable in that kind of system. Also, now I can realize the importance of the training at the Academy. At the time, it seemed stupid to memorize menus and other information when there wasn't enough time to do it. We had to do that under deliberate pressure from the upperclassmen. But then, when I was out over the North Atlantic with 20 passengers in a helicopter, knowing that going down in that cold water would end our lives in minutes, I knew that a split-second reaction using a memorized emergency checklist could make the difference between living and dying. That's the way it is in the military; your decisions and your reactions don't just lose money as in the business world; when things go wrong in the military, people's lives are on the line and whether they live or die can depend upon your ability to perform.

...when things go wrong in the military, people's lives are on the line and whether they live or die can depend upon your ability to perform.

There is a rationale behind the stress and pressure you experience at the Academy. So, it's an individual decision whether or not you want to become an individual who can handle that. But let me say this: the good part of it is that you develop confidence in yourself after those kinds of experiences. And self confidence is a key component to success in any field.

Flying was in my blood. My grandfather, who was in the Class of 1930, flew in several campaigns in the Pacific during World War II, and my father, Class of 1951, was a test pilot and fighter pilot in the Vietnam War. My dream was to become an astronaut—an impossible dream when I started at the Academy the summer of 1977, but a reality 15 years later.

Of course, I have to add one more thing. For me there is a lot of satisfaction knowing that I'm serving my country, especially after it has given so much to me. I don't make a big thing out of it, but that makes me feel good about myself and makes me believe that what I'm doing goes beyond my personal sense of accomplishment.

Lieutenant Marilisa Gibellato Elrod, Class of 1996.

Lieutenant Elrod ran track, played soccer, and was on the gymnastics team at the Naval Academy. She earned one of a limited number of slots to medical school on graduation, and was also selected as a Marshall Scholar to study in Great Britain. So she put med school on hold, earned a natural sciences degree, then went to medical school at Ohio State. She earned both a PhD in biostatistics and a medical degree before returning to active duty with the Navy. She is now an undersea medical doctor assigned to the Naval Submarine Support Command in Pearl Harbor, HI.

Lt. Elrod at Navy dive school.
MARILISA GIBELLATO ELROD

My grandfather is a World War II vet, a former Navy pilot. He tried to convince my older brother to go to the Naval Academy, and I overheard their conversations. I started looking into it, met the fantastic track coaches and got interested. I think it was the challenge and the academic reputation that attracted me. I'm also a very active and service minded person, and I thought I would fit in well.

You can read about what the Academy is like, talk to people and do all your research, and still not know what you're getting into. I was surprised by how hard I had to work, and by how talented everyone else was. All of us had a pretty easy go of it in high school, so it was a bit of a shock for everyone.

What I liked most about the Academy was the people. My classmates were just fantastic—the nicest, most accepting, most helpful people I've ever met. I liked being around people like myself, academically motivated, adventurous, people you have a lot of things in common with, people you will keep in touch with all your life.

Sports have always been a big part of my life, and sports were probably what got me through the Academy—the friendships I made, having time away from the Academy environment, especially time with just my female teammates. Some women at the academy shy away from female friendships because they think it will separate them from the guys, but those friendships can really get you through some hard times.

After graduation, my plan was to go to medical school. I was a finalist for both Rhodes and Marshall Scholarships, and I received the Marshall Scholarship offered through the British government. So the Navy allowed me to postpone medical school. I spent two years as a Marshall Scholar at Cambridge University studying virology, then went to medical school at Ohio State, which was close to home. During med school, I would spend about six weeks each year in uniform, performing Navy medical research or different military hospital rotations.

After my internship in pediatrics at Bethesda's National Naval Medical Center, I went to six months of training to become an undersea medical officer. I went through Navy dive school as part of that training, and now my job is to treat submariners and decide whether they can go underway with the sub. I also ride the subs occasionally to check in with the corpsmen who work under my medical license, to make sure the patients are receiving optimal care.

One of the ways the Academy helped me became obvious to me in medical school, and that's the importance of having balance to your life, always making time for everything that's important. The Academy teaches you to manage your time and multitask. I noticed a lot of students in med school were good students but really didn't have good life balance. I did well, but I also had a very full life. I was involved in many other things and made time for my family, so I think I had a better experience than some of my classmates.

If you're applying to the Naval Academy, make sure you have the proper motivation.

Another lesson from the Academy that I apply every day has to do with the strength of character and integrity that they emphasize. As a physician, it's incredibly important to have your patients trust you. They have to know you'll maintain confidentiality and do what's best for them.

I also learned to take advantage of every opportunity that's presented. Don't waste any opportunities to get further schooling. It might be training—it's not always a degree. But the Academy and the Navy taught me that you really have to jump on those opportunities when they're presented. You might worry that it will add to your workload, but I've learned that it's worth the extra effort.

If you're applying to the Naval Academy, make sure you have the proper motivation. Don't go to the Academy because someone else wants you to, or because of the money you'll save, but because you want to be an officer. If you're struggling with your goals, it's not an easy place to be.

The Academy is an excellent place to go if you have a strong sense of service. Whether you have a goal to be career military, or you're someone who wants to be involved in government or public service in general, it's a great place. The Academy will also help you if you end up going into civilian business. You will deal with the same mix of people—very successful people like your classmates.

My advice for new plebes is to make sure you're in good physical and mental shape. Be prepared physically; do a lot of running. You also need to be prepared mentally. Arrive having come to terms with your decision to go to the Naval Academy. Some plebes are still mourning the loss of that "normal college experience." Be at peace with your choice, and know there are so many opportunities that will come because of it.

Clint Bruce, Class of 1997

Clint Bruce was a four-year varsity linebacker for the Navy football team. After graduation, he successfully completed the demanding training to become a member of the elite Navy SEALs.[5] He led special operations units during the war on terrorism before leaving the Navy for the civilian world. He held a job in the finance sector, and was hired to rescue more than 900 people from New Orleans during the Hurricane Katrina crisis. Based on that experience, he founded a company that provides global intelligence, security, and disaster response services for businesses.

I knew about the SEAL teams before I knew about the Naval Academy, and I was really intrigued by that community. I started getting recruited to play college football, and my father took me to see a game at the Naval

Clint Bruce's business takes him all over the world.   Clint Bruce

---

5. SEALs are named for their ability to conduct special operations from the sea, air, or land.

Academy, so my knowledge of that opportunity became clearer. The LeapFrogs (Navy SEAL Parachute Team) jumped into that game and I had an opportunity to meet some of the SEALs and to ask some questions and get some "real deal" answers.

I probably had opportunities to play football for a Big 12 school, but I shut them all down pretty quickly. I knew the Academy gave me an opportunity to support my family. My father was ill, and I knew if I blew out my knee at someplace like the University of Texas, we didn't have money for me to go to school without a football scholarship.

My dad was able to help me to understand the benefits of attending one of the most prestigious institutions in this country, one that will have an impact for the rest of your life. Dad was a businessman and helped me understand the legitimacy you gain having the Naval Academy as part of your resume.

My father died on June 27th, 1992, and I reported to the Naval Academy Prep School just a few weeks after that. That period in my life was a bit surreal, but the structure that the Prep School imposed on me was very important in retrospect. Had I not had that imposed activity and discipline, I don't know if I would have been successful.

You have to be able to think and learn and be able to deal with the challenges.

Academically, the Naval Academy is as competitive as the NFL is physically. In high school I was smart enough to do well without trying hard. Then everyone shows up and they've always been the best, and now they're surrounded by other people who have always been the best. The demands of the class load, the intellect required to be successful, was a real wakeup for me. That's a good lesson for the real world. You have to be able to think and learn and be able to deal with the challenges. All four years, I struggled to balance academics and athletics. That was part of my growing and maturing as a young man.

Good roommates were critical for me. They always helped me when I was struggling academically. I think it's nice to be around people who are smarter than you. For me at Annapolis, that wasn't hard—all I had to do was walk out in the hall! That's another life lesson—you can succeed by surrounding yourself with people better than you and learning from them. I also leaned on my sponsor family. They're still my family; I talk to them all the time.

Becoming a SEAL was harder than I thought it would be. I had to compete with my classmates just to have the opportunity to try to become a SEAL.[6] At Coronado, we started with 162 in our BUD/S class, and graduated 12 of the original 162. Five of them were Naval Academy grads—

6. Bruce had to compete with 250 other midshipmen for just 16 slots to attend BUD/S.

they were some of the most incredible men I have ever had the opportunity to serve and suffer with.

There wasn't a BUD/S instructor I was more afraid of than the strength coach at the Naval Academy. I think I was uniquely prepared for BUD/S having been an athlete at the Naval Academy. I had learned how to fit 32 hours of work into a 24 hour day. I had learned time management and survival skills. Being acclimated to an adversarial environment, to crappy conditions, helped. I have a saying: "You gotta love it when it sucks." I was used to that. BUD/S wasn't the first time I had to struggle through an injury, get up early, and do more things than I possibly had time for.

I had the opportunity to play in the NFL [with the Ravens and Saints], but the Navy needed me to serve. For about five minutes, I was mad. But everything I was able to do as a SEAL, the men I was able to work with, you can't buy that experience anywhere. Peyton Manning will buy drinks for a military man every day, just to hear their stories. Football is just a game. I loved it, but now that I have kids I can recognize the significance of my contributions. It's humbling to say I was part of the Navy and the SEALs.

I got to see the world, too. There were heroic, storybook things I got to see people do, especially the enlisted sailors and soldiers—if anyone has any doubts about this generation, if you could see what they'll do, how smart and heroic and selfless they are, you'd have no doubt that we're in good hands.

In the Navy, I got life experience that's irreplaceable. As a 23-year-old in the Navy, you will find yourself in charge of millions of dollars and the lives of other men. Your mistakes are real world mistakes. The leadership and officership you learn will give you instant credibility in the business community. A 60-year-old multi-millionaire will take you seriously.

Looking back, I always knew I wanted to serve. My folks had raised me that way. When I talk to young people about the Academy and the Navy, if they don't have part of them that believes there's something more important than themselves, I don't have much time for them. You have to go in with a heart for service. I don't understand people who think the cost of freedom is not worth paying, or that freedom has no cost other than taxes.

My advice for making it through the Naval Academy is to remember what you wanted to do when you signed up. There will be times that the certainty of reaching the end state and graduating gets challenged by the discomfort of the moment. Always remember why you were there and what you wanted to do, look past the moment … and get where you wanted to go.

HOW TO PREPARE

FOUR
Mental Preparation Comes First

Throughout this book you will hear midshipmen and graduates talk about the challenges of the Naval Academy—the difficult and highly technical academic load, the physical demands, and the exacting military training. If the Naval Academy is so hard, how do so many midshipmen survive all four years and graduate?

When you talk to Naval Academy graduates, nearly all of them will tell you that mental preparation is the most important factor to making it through. If your mind is properly prepared, all of the stress and all of the challenges will be easier for you to endure. If your mind is not prepared, then you will wake up each day questioning why you are there. You will meet each challenge thinking about your family back home or your friends at State U. If you do not have the right mindset, you will be miserable, and you will most likely come face to face with something new: failure.

Those who fail are usually those who have not mentally prepared themselves.

GOALS: THE RIGHT MOTIVATION TO SUCCEED

Those who lose sight of their goals, or who never had the right ones in the first place, are usually the first to fall. To survive, you MUST have unwavering goals. You MUST have reasons, good reasons, not to give up. One midshipman put it this way: "I think a lot of people quit because they just don't know why they're here. They start to question that and it just gets to be too much, and they just want to go home."

The reasons young men and women choose the Naval Academy are individual and complex. But after conducting hundreds of interviews, some common motives began to appear again and again. We will examine each of them and see if any of them might create problems for you.

I want a free, quality education

This is a good reason to go to the Academy. The Naval Academy is considered an outstanding academic institution with superb professors, receiving top ratings in nation-wide surveys. Those who want a rigorous education, especially in engineering, are seldom disappointed. But even the most enthusiastic scholars have to divide their attention between academic, military, and physical demands. So if you want to focus solely on your education, a traditional college may be a better choice. Also, if you want to be highly specialized in one field of study, you may find the Academy's large and diverse core curriculum is not for you. The Academy education is

The education at the Naval Academy is not really free; it comes at a cost. USNA Photo Lab

designed to prepare well-rounded leaders for military service.

You must also realize that the education really is not free. You have to earn that education with hard work and complete dedication of your body and mind. Also, you become obligated for that "free" education.

If you graduate, you are obligated to serve on active duty in the Navy or Marine Corps for five years. Some specialized training, such as flight school, comes with an even longer commitment. Of course, you should also realize that these required terms of duty can change at any time, even while you are in the Academy.

Nine years—four years at the Academy and five as a naval officer—may seem like an enormous amount of time when you are only 17 years old. Of course, you will be compensated with money and benefits during all those years, and the pay could be about what you would make after graduating from a civilian college. You will also see the world and gain experiences you cannot find elsewhere. But you will be expected to perform whatever job you are assigned to the best of your ability, and live wherever the Navy assigns you. You cannot just quit as you might in a civilian job.

I want a challenge

Midshipmen repeatedly cited the challenge as something that attracted them to the Naval Academy. Some like the discipline and military training—a few even said they wished it were tougher. Others wanted a tough and well-respected academic experience. These are smart, competitive people who never felt pushed or challenged in high school. They want to take on something difficult to prove to themselves they can do it, learn their strengths and limitations, and make themselves better.

For those who come deliberately seeking a challenge, few are disappointed. Midshipmen must learn to use every minute wisely and juggle many tasks under constant pressure. If the basic requirements are not challenging enough, they can take on a double major, become leaders within the Brigade, or get involved in extra-curricular activities. Surrounded by other equally capable, equally competitive young men and women, they often find they push one another to work even harder. The Naval Academy is an ideal place for those who want to find their own limits and be pushed to do their best.

I want to play Division I sports

The Academy may offer an opportunity to play NCAA Division I varsity sports that a student would not have at a civilian college. The Academy must recruit candidates who are not only competitive athletes, but who also have strong academic records, demonstrated leadership ability, and a commitment to serve their country. Ohio State and UCLA have a much broader pool from which to recruit.

Athletes must understand (or learn quickly) that regardless how dedicated they are as athletes, the Naval Academy's mission is to turn them into naval officers. Their chances to play professional sports are nearly nonexistent, and practicing their sport must fit into a schedule jammed with academic and military responsibilities. However, for athletes who want to play in a superb program while getting an outstanding education and a guaranteed job, the Naval Academy is a good place to be.

My father/mother/grandparents want me to go

Many sad tales were heard during our interviews. The majority of them were about midshipmen who found themselves at the Academy living out someone else's dream. This is definitely a bad reason to go to the Academy. Perhaps they had a parent or grandparent who graduated from the Naval Academy who is eager to see the family tradition go on. Perhaps their mother or father sees the Naval Academy as a way out of paying college tuition, or an opportunity so good that no one should pass it up.

Nearly every group of midshipmen, when asked about their classmates who quit, cited an example of someone who came because mom or dad wanted them to. These situations almost never have happy endings. Said one, "I saw people leaving, people who didn't want to be here. They had their parents sort of force it upon them and they just weren't into it." Most agreed that you can tough it out if you are there for yourself, but it is too hard to do for someone else.

The saddest tale of all came from a blue and gold officer who graduated in the 1980s.[1] She remembered a midshipman whose small town held a parade in his honor when he got his nomination—he had not even received his appointment yet. The dreams of the whole town were poured into this one unfortunate young man.

---

1. Blue and gold officers are representatives of the Academy Admissions Office. Their role is discussed in Chapter 9.

When he got to the Academy, he began to question his motives for being there. When he called home, his parents told him the family could not endure the shame if he quit. The midshipman struggled awhile longer before realizing the Naval Academy didn't mesh with his personality and career ambitions, and he decided to quit anyway. He was last seen sitting in the hallway of Bancroft Hall, surrounded by boxes of personal belongings from home, figuring out his next step. He had been disowned by his family.

The blue and gold officer who related this story has developed techniques for discovering candidates who are being pushed by others to apply. Most blue and gold officers and congressional nomination panels are constantly on the lookout for overenthusiastic parents of underenthusiastic candidates. They usually offer a private, one-on-one opportunity for the candidate to bow out—such a candidate will not be offered an appointment and the parents will never know why.

I want to go for the glamour and recognition

This is a bad reason, but who would admit to it? Nobody, probably. But young people can get caught up in their egos without ever realizing that it is happening. A typical example is the student who says to a teacher or counselor at school, "Oh, I'm thinking about the Naval Academy as a possible college."

"The Naval Academy! Oh, that's a wonderful idea!" is the excited reply. "You are bright and have all the other qualities. Go for it. Now here's

Those who come for the challenge are seldom disappointed. Those who come for the glamour usually quit.   USNA PHOTO LAB

all you have to do to get the process started..." It is certainly a prestigious school with a long tradition and famous, successful alumni.

One thing leads to another and the student gets swept up in the process—and all the new attention feeds the ego. Letters start arriving from the Academy. There are telephone calls from the local blue and gold officer, and perhaps even a call from the Academy itself. All that is heady stuff for a high school kid.

Then there is the contact with a congressman or senator and a follow-up letter. More heady stuff, for how many times does a high school student even get letters?

Now the pressure is mounting. Something that seemed like a good idea just to explore is now a steam roller picking up momentum. And the student, while perhaps having doubts, does not want to disappoint those who are now working hard to help him. So the student's determination grows, because who wants to be a failure at this point?

Next come the hurdles: the medical examination, the physical fitness test and the interviews. Facing those challenges the student says to himself, "Hey, I'm no wimp. I'm going to make it. I'm going to show these people that I've got the right stuff."

And he makes it. Suddenly he really has the RIGHT STUFF because he is ACCEPTED! And just so he will believe he has the right stuff, all he has to do is read the local newspaper where his honor is announced, or watch the audience at graduation as they applaud his magnificent achievement.

Then what? Plebe Summer and detailers screaming in your face. The academic year starts and you are starved for sleep and struggling to pass your classes for the first time in your life. You are constantly being criticized and corrected. This is the glamorous life you had envisioned?

Nobody wants to admit that they are at the Academy for glamour and recognition. They end up embarrassed and demoralized...and they usually quit.

I want to be a naval officer

This is the best reason of all, IF you know WHY you want to be an officer. The complete four year Academy program is valued at nearly $350,000. Those taxpayer dollars are intended to be an investment in a career officer.

Try answering the following questions. If you say "yes" to most of them, you are mentally prepared with the best reasons for going to the Academy.

- Do you want to serve your country and defend its freedoms? Are you prepared to go wherever the nation needs you, even into combat?
- Do you enjoy the challenges of leadership?
- Do you want heavy responsibility at a much younger age than you could expect in a civilian job?

- Do you want to become a better person?
- Do you respect the traditions of the Naval Academy?
- Do you want to be a naval officer so you can serve aboard a ship or submarine, or become a Marine or a pilot?
- Do you look forward to the challenge of a new assignment every three or four years instead of just one lifelong job?
- Do you want more job security than you would have in most civilian jobs?
- Do you want to be able to retire at an age young enough to start another career?

In summary, there are GOOD REASONS and BAD REASONS for going to the Naval Academy. The first step in getting your mind prepared for the Academy is to know that you are going for the GOOD REASONS.

If you are going for the BAD REASONS, consider doing yourself a favor by stopping right now. If you do not, you can expect to have an unhappy, and perhaps short, career as a midshipman.

KNOW WHAT TO EXPECT

The second thing you should do in preparing your mind for the Academy is to know what to expect when you get there.

A skipper getting ready to take his ship out on a cruise will spend months getting his Sailors ready to go. Part of that process includes finding out what to expect. What mission will the crew undertake, and where will they go? What threats and weather conditions will they face?

When you get ready to take on four years at the Naval Academy, you must also do your homework so you understand what kinds of waters you will be navigating. Reading this book is a good first step. But there are several other things that are recommended.

Meet your blue and gold officer. Every high school in the nation has a blue and gold officer (details in Chapter 9). If your counselor does not know how to contact yours, contact the Naval Academy Admissions Office.

Search for other naval officers who will talk with you. They are almost always eager to advise students, especially the retired officers who have extra time. Tell the officer on your first contact that you are thinking about applying to the Academy and you are wondering what being an officer is really like. At the interview ask the hard questions, such as, What are the worst things about being a naval officer? What happens when an officer does not get promoted? If officers make a mistake, what happens to them?

Another thing you should do is discuss the Academy with one or more midshipmen while they are home on vacation. If you do not know of any, just contact your counselor or blue and gold officer, and he or she will help connect you.

If the typical college environment appeals to you, go to a typical college. As one midshipman explained, "When I decided to come here, I knew I was going to get yelled at. My roommate stayed for a semester and realized that it wasn't what he wanted to do because he was the party animal guy in high school. He had all the friends, and he stayed in contact with all of them. He just couldn't handle them having all the fun and being left out."

The BEST thing for you to do is VISIT THE NAVAL ACADEMY. When you get there, you will see what Academy life is like, talk to midshipmen and staff, and try to picture yourself there. You can compete to attend the week-long Summer Seminar (see www.usna.edu/Admissions/nass.htm), attend a sports camp (http://navysports.cstv.com/camps/navy-camps.html), or arrange a visit with the Admissions Office. These programs are discussed in more detail in Chapter 8.

The midshipmen who visited the Academy before going there all said that it helped them because they knew what to expect. A visit also shows your blue and gold officer and congressional interview panel that you are committed and enthusiastic enough about attending the Academy that you are willing to do some homework on your own.

Some candidates decide NOT to apply after a visit, but that is fine—the Naval Academy and you are better off if you learn that the Naval Academy is not for you before you accept an appointment.

DETERMINATION

Mental preparation for the Academy must include one more task. That task is to convince yourself that you are going to succeed when you get there. You cannot be a quitter.

Thousands and thousands of graduates before you have made it through. If you made it through the competitive admissions process, you DO have what it takes to succeed, if you are willing to work hard, and if you are determined.

Tips in this book and advice from your classmates will help you get through the hard times. But only if you resolve to make it through before you start Plebe Summer.

You must decide that you are not a quitter.
USNA PHOTO LAB

If you do realize that the Naval Academy is really not the right place for you, I recommend you resolve to make it through your plebe year before you leave. By sticking it out for a full year, you will benefit several ways:

First, you will come away with college credits you can transfer to just about any school in the nation. You will also have learned more about yourself than you would as a freshman at another college.

If you stay through the first year, you will never doubt whether you could have made it. You can be assured that you are leaving on your own terms.

At the end of the year, something else might happen: you might change your mind. You might realize the worst is behind you and the rest is not so bad after all. You might become so close to your classmates that you want to stay with them and serve alongside them. You might realize that Annapolis and the Navy are exactly where you belong.

A final note: Many midshipmen said they had thought about quitting at some time, either seriously or just as a passing thought on a particularly bad day. Not one of them said they regretted the decision to stay.

FIVE
Why Many Plebes Suffer
Academic Shock

After breezing through high school with minimum effort, being told how smart they are, most midshipmen are quickly humbled when they start taking academic classes at the Naval Academy. They are shocked to find themselves struggling as they never have before.

What is the problem? Why should midshipmen who have scored high on ACT and SAT tests, and graduated near the top of their high school classes, encounter so much trouble with course work at the Academy?

There are at least seven reasons, many of which can be traced back to habits formed in high school.

PROBLEM ONE: COMPETITION

Remember the words of Clint Bruce in Chapter 3? He equated academics at the Naval Academy to the physical competition in the NFL. Most of the midshipmen who come to the Academy have been the top students in their high schools. Recent classes have entered with average SAT scores over 1,300. And they became top students through a competitive process that enabled them to rise above others in their school who were less gifted or motivated.

But how much competition did they really have? Most took classes with students with all ranges of abilities and motivation. Many midshipmen said that they were able to get good grades in high school without much effort. Several admitted that they just listened in class and relied on their natural learning ability. They relied on the teacher to make sure they understood the material, not on themselves.

Now try to imagine what happens when all of these "good" students get into classes together at the Academy. Suddenly the competitive situation is drastically different. The competition is now fierce, and a large number of former "good" students end up on the bottom half of the grade curve. Students who were use to seeing easy grades of "A" are suddenly looking at "D's" or worse.

PROBLEM TWO: OVERLOAD

Most high school students, even the overachievers who receive appointments to service academies, do not experience much stress getting their school work done. Even with extracurricular activities, sports, or a part-time job, finding enough hours to do all you need to has not been a real challenge. At the Naval Academy, that will change.

Besides taking 18-20 semester hours of challenging courses (compared to perhaps 15 hours their civilian counterparts must take), a midshipman has mandatory athletic and military training every day. During the plebe year, many midshipmen will discover that the techniques that worked in high school do not work at the Naval Academy.

They may procrastinate, as they did in high school, until the night before a big assignment or paper is due. Then they realize they have other things that have to get done, or the assignment takes longer than they expected. The result is a poorly-done assignment completed at 2 a.m., and a midshipman who cannot stay awake in class the next day.

Or they resolve to do every assignment for the next day to the best of their ability, read every word on every page, and even spend extra time on material that is giving them trouble. Using that approach in high school meant they got top grades in their classes. But by midnight their brain is begging for sleep, and they still have two of their four assignments left to do.

Many midshipmen talked about the importance—and challenge—of balancing academics and the many other demands on their time. Succeeding academically means figuring out how to strike that balance. Throughout this book, you will read advice about how to do that.

PROBLEM THREE: LETTER HUNTERS

If you are now a student, look around during one of your classes, then ask yourself this question: What do these students, myself included, really want out of this class? If you are objective, you will probably come up with this answer: "A's" or maybe "B's."

Are you a letter hunter? Or are you really trying to learn the material? In chemistry class do you really want to understand the significance of Avogadro's Number? In history class do you really want to know how the Missouri Compromise affected the next one hundred years of life in America? In advanced algebra class do you really want to know how quadratic equations can help you solve a whole new class of problems?

Or are you memorizing all those things just long enough to get the letters that you want? Many "good" students are letter hunters. They do whatever is necessary to get the first letter or two in the alphabet. Then they go on to the next letter-hunting challenge. They are often more concerned about pleasing the teacher who assigns the grade than they are about learning the material being taught. As a result, sometimes they do not learn much at all.

So what awaits a "good" student when professors at the Academy expect a midshipman to have high school-level knowledge of algebra or history or chemistry? Just having good grades from high school will not cut it. The professors at the Academy are not interested in your high school letters. They ARE interested in building on knowledge that you were supposed to have gained during your high school years.

So be warned. Those who go to an Academy class with just letters, rather than knowledge, had better expect some hard times.

PROBLEM FOUR: ESCAPE ARTISTS

Many "good" high school students have a bag of tricks they can use to escape detection when they come to class unprepared. Some look at their desks and remain silent if volunteers are asked to answer questions. This works especially well in large classes. It is easy to vanish in the crowd.

Another trick is leave the textbook open and scan the lesson rapidly before the teacher begins asking questions. This is a favorite of those who are good readers.

One of the best tricks, when the teacher is not alert, is to listen carefully to what the teacher has said and then volunteer when one of the questions has an obvious answer. That gets the student off the hook, usually for the whole class period. After dodging one bullet, a student is not likely to get shot at again, especially in a big class.

If you happen to be a "good" student, you can probably add your own favorite techniques to this list. Students have probably been creating them forever. But realize that you might as well leave your bag of tricks at home if you go to the Naval Academy.

Why? Because the classes are small—about 18 students on average—and every professor will know your name and something about you within a day or two after you start a class. Moreover, your professors believe strongly in ACCOUNTABILITY.

This means that they will hold you responsible for whatever reading or homework they assigned. More important, unlike your high school teachers who were burdened with large student loads, they will do some kind of accounting that will let them know how well you did your assignment.

That might be a quiz. It might be a barrage of questions that you cannot escape. It might even be a trip to the front of the class or to the board so your knowledge, or lack of it, can be displayed for the whole class.

Escape artists do not do well at the Academy. In small classes with determined professors, there is no way to dodge the bullets. And if you try, you are sure to get wounded.

PROBLEM FIVE: COPIERS

Some "good" students are able to get the grades they want in high school by cheating. But they present little problem at the Academy because midshipmen with that kind of character rarely survive.

The "copiers" who do have problems at the Academy are not necessarily cheaters, at least not intentionally. On the contrary, they are often very conscientious students.

Are you a "copier?" Here is how to tell. What do you do if your teacher gives a reading assignment and also asks that you write out the answers to certain questions that are at the end of the chapter?

Do you read the assignment two or three times, or whatever it takes to understand it thoroughly? Then do you write out the answers to the questions in your own words, thinking as you write, and taking pride in your good grammar, punctuation and spelling? And finally, do you proofread your answers to make sure you gave the best possible answer, free of errors?

If so, pat yourself on the back and consider yourself unique. You will probably do well at the Naval Academy.

Or do you answer the questions by simply copying the relevant sentence or two from the assigned chapter? Do you finish the homework without even thinking about what you just wrote, or how it relates to other lessons in the same class?

A very important part of an officer's job is writing reports. So writing is required in most classes...

Some high school teachers even encourage this kind of copying. It is much easier to grade the homework or a test if they see the familiar words right out of the textbook.

How do you go about writing a paper? Do you cut and paste whole sentences and even paragraphs word-for-word right off of a web site? Of course, the serious letter hunters will not stop at that. They also will copy something from an additional web site or maybe even a library book, "just to be safe."

The problem with copiers is that they have not learned how to organize their thoughts, synthesize multiple ideas into new ideas, and write them in a logical, systematic manner. This is a serious handicap at the Academy because there is a heavy emphasis on developing just that skill.

A very important part of an officer's job is writing reports. So writing is required in most classes—not just in English classes—and a student who has been a copier is in immediate trouble with such assignments. Midshipmen are expected to synthesize and understand what they have read, not just copy it. Even more seriously, if a copier at the Naval Academy fails to acknowledge his or her sources, it may constitute cheating, an Honor Concept violation which can result in dismissal.

Writing cannot be learned without practice. The copier has to get that practice at the worst possible time—when all the other pressures on the first-year midshipman are at their maximum.

PROBLEM SIX: SENIORITIS

Teachers who love teaching, who would never want to do anything else, who think it is the greatest job in the world, seldom like teaching seniors during their final semester in high school.

The reason: senioritis, a behavior pattern where seniors coast through the last weeks of school with the least effort possible.

Many excuses are used to justify such behavior. "I'm burned out on school." "I have worked long enough; now I want to play." "I just can't get going any more." "I already got accepted to the college I want to go to."

Have you heard any of those excuses? You will if you are not yet a senior. But just remember, if you are planning on going to the Naval Academy, senioritis is a serious affliction.

During the senior year, high school students have the opportunity to take the kinds of classes that will help them the most at the Academy. This is the year when high-level math, science or English courses can be taken. This is the year when creative writing is most likely to be an elective. This is the year when Advanced Placement college courses are available. Most important, this is the time when one's learning curve and study habits should be PEAKING, not declining.

Students who hit the Academy running and in peak form suffer less stress than those who are out of shape mentally. If you are lazy your senior year in high school, beware. The Academy is likely to be harder on you than for those who managed to escape the problem.

PROBLEM SEVEN: SIT-AND-GET LEARNING

Sit-and-get learners are the product of a type of teaching common in high schools. Smart high school students, the kind of students who become candidates for a service academy, are often very successful with this kind of learning. And high school teachers are often their accomplices. The students sit in class like an empty cup into which the teacher pours knowledge until the cup is sufficiently full.

Consider the following classroom scenario: The teacher, Mr. Spoonfeeder, assigns a chapter in the science textbook on Monday. On Tuesday, he reviews all the material from that chapter that he feels is important—those things he will cover on the test. He will explain it in great detail, and because he is a conscientious teacher, he will then ask questions to make sure the students understand it.

The next day, he will hand out worksheets in class, watching as his students complete all the questions. If anyone has a question, he is right there to explain the concept again and help the student get to the right answer.

On Thursday, he decides that the concepts were awfully difficult and most of the students are struggling. So he works hard to come up with another method of explaining the lesson, to ensure everyone grasps it. On

You must take responsibility for learning and understanding what it taught.

USNA PHOTO LAB

Friday, he reviews sample test questions in class, just to make absolutely sure the students are ready for the test.

Most midshipmen will come to the Academy having had teachers like this. They have been spoonfed for years by conscientious teachers who believed that they were doing what was best for their students. The smarter students know that if they do not grasp the material the first time it is presented, Mr. Spoonfeeder will surely explain it again. All they have to do is keep coming to class and paying attention, and Mr. Spoonfeeder will make sure they learn what they need to know. Unfortunately, those students never had the opportunity to learn HOW TO LEARN on their own.

And what do they find at the Academy?

Professor Independence. The faculty is loaded with them. Those professors give assignments and hold midshipmen accountable for knowing AND understanding the material the minute they arrive in class. They will move on quickly, and any midshipman who does not grasp the concepts taught will have to ask for extra help OUTSIDE of class. If they do not, they will be left behind.

Why? Because they have to do it to train the kinds of officers needed by the Navy and Marine Corps.

Naval officers must be efficient, independent learners in order to keep on top of rapidly-evolving technology and operate in a dynamic world. The professors at the Naval Academy will expect you to develop the appetite and ability to learn—and understand—complex ideas. Lives will depend on you. That is why they teach the way they do.

So you should not be surprised by the difficulty of the academic load at the Naval Academy. But how can you be prepared for those academic challenges?

A NEW ATTITUDE TOWARD LEARNING

If you still have a year or more left of your high school career, the best advice is to CHANGE YOUR ATTITUDE.

Change your attitude about competition. If there is little competition in your classes, pretend that you are in a class with students who are all as capable as you. Get in the habit of always doing more than you are assigned. Learn to take pride in giving 150 percent effort in the classroom.

You are probably an athlete of some kind. Bring your competitive attitude from the playing field into the classroom. Take pride in never letting up. Treat your course work like an opponent. Master it, not just halfway, but completely.

Also, you should change your attitude about what you want to get out of your classes. Despite what has been said about letter hunting, there is nothing wrong with getting good grades. In fact, you have to have good grades just to be accepted at the Academy. But letter hunting should not be your MAIN goal. Your main goal should be learning the material in your courses.

If you will do that, and you do it well, and you really try to remember what you have learned, the good letters will come. You do not sacrifice anything by going after knowledge rather than letters. Instead, you get a two-fer: you get the knowledge AND the letters.

Are you an escape artist? If you are the type of person who continually wants to slide by without doing assigned work, your tricks might get you into the Academy but you will not last. If you are that type of person, the upperclassmen and professors will find you out. They will make sure you do not survive long enough to create problems as a naval officer.

Do you even need to be told that you should quit copying your reports and answers to questions out of books?

If you are going through the motions of completing a homework assignment without learning a thing, you are going about it the wrong way. So bite the bullet. Start writing material out of your head instead of out of a book. The effort might be painful at first. But it has never been known to cause brain damage. Your brain is like your muscles—it has to be in shape for you to succeed at the Naval Academy.

Will you catch senioritis? This is a problem you can avoid if you are determined. How? By deliberately taking the hardest courses you can during your senior year and developing a special attitude about those courses.

Believe that they are more important than anything else you have taken in high school. Then go after them with determination.

Learn everything that there is to learn in those courses, and more. Once you have committed yourself to this kind of effort, you will not have time to catch senioritis. And when you get to the Academy, you will have one less problem to worry about.

What if you are a sit-and-get learner? Your main problem, if you are still in high school, is that you cannot control the methods that your teachers use. And you are not likely to find many Professor Independences in your high school. But you are not helpless. Be as prepared as you can possibly be. Even make it a game to try to know more about the subject than the teacher knows, or keep track of everything the teacher says that you didn't already know.

HOW TO PREPARE ACADEMICALLY

Besides developing the proper attitude about learning, what else should you do to prepare for the Academy?

You should take all of the math courses that are available in your high school. Take four years of English and four years of a foreign language if that is possible. Take chemistry and physics—advanced courses if you can.

Take computer courses. All midshipmen are issued a computer, and you will find that your computer is used to manage nearly every aspect of your life. You may have to e-mail a homework assignment to your instructor, use a computer-aided design program for an engineering project, or collaborate on line to complete a team project. If you are not comfortable using most common computer programs, you will add to your workload and stress level. If you can take some programming classes, you will have an advantage in the challenging computer science class.

Many candidates for the Academy take Advanced Placement, or AP, classes. Most midshipmen and instructors will tell you those AP classes will help you validate core courses or have an easier time in the first semester or two. One word of caveat: Make sure you actually learn what the AP classes teach, and remember the material in the classes leading up to the AP class. Take AP Calculus as an example. You must come to the Academy with a good, working comprehension of the algebra and trigonometry you took in high school. And if you test out of Calculus 1 and go immediately to Calculus 2, you must retain, understand, and be able to apply all you were supposed to have learned. All the warnings at the beginning of this chapter apply.

Speech is an excellent course if you have room in your schedule for an elective. The practice of speaking before a group builds confidence. And it gives you practice thinking on your feet. You will appreciate that experience if you go to the Academy because you will have to stand up and speak in front of your peers.

If you are a slow reader, a reading class that teaches speed, comprehension, and recall will be a great investment. Plowing through several hundred pages a night is not unusual. Being an efficient reader will help you get through all your assignments and still get a reasonable night's sleep.

A final bit of advice has to do with study techniques. Each night, before you start studying, look over all the assignments. Quickly turn through the pages of your textbooks and try to estimate how long it should take you to do each assignment. Then give yourself a time allotment for each one. Leave time, also, for breaks and phone calls. Later, when you finish studying, give yourself a grade on how closely your study time matched your estimates.

Try the above for a few weeks, then start pushing yourself. Estimate the time needed for your assignments and for your breaks. Then try to shorten the study time by pretending that you have other things to do. But do not eliminate the breaks. Short breaks are essential.

Get in the habit of planning your entire week, looking ahead at upcoming papers, projects, tests, and quizzes. Schedule time for each one, and try to stick to the schedule.

This is realistic study practice, because at the Academy your assignments will be long and the time to do them will be limited. You will rarely have enough time to study as much as you would like. You will have to prioritize and make compromises. By learning to do that in high school, you will have one less thing to learn in the high-pressure environment of the Academy.

SUCCESS STORY:
COMMANDER (retired) DOUG DENNENY, Class of 1984

At age 16, I knew I wanted to fly, so I was looking at the Air Force Academy and the Naval Academy. I chose the Naval Academy because I knew that if I decided not to fly, I'd have other good options. At a service academy I knew I would get a great education, improve myself, then serve my country ... it would kick start my life.

Academics were much harder than I expected. I went out for crew my first semester, and it was so physically demanding that I was completely exhausted. I was always amazed at the midshipmen who could do it all. But I was an NCAA athlete, a plebe, an aerospace engineering major, and I was physically wiped out every night. I couldn't study any longer and I couldn't do it all. So I didn't do very well academically my first semester.

I had to meet an academic board [to determine if he would face disenrollment], and my coach had written a positive endorsement. He thought I could continue to do crew AND bring my grades up, and so did the board. But when they asked me what I was going to do differently the next semester, I knew the answer was to quit crew.

I grew up a lot my plebe year. I learned that you could not be satisfied with not completely understanding a concept that was taught in class. Based on my experience in high school, I always thought, "It'll become clear later on; I'll figure it out later." But I soon learned that if you didn't understand every concept, it would show up on the test and you would be punished for it.

You had better figure it out pretty quickly because the next day they will move on, and the concepts will build on what you were supposed to have learned. So you have to ask the question, or hope your roommate understands better than you. We had a saying: cooperate and graduate. You found people in your academic major who understood the lesson, then went to their room and asked them to explain it.

My grades shot up second semester, and I graduated with an aerospace engineering degree. But first I had to learn time management. When you get to the Naval Academy, your days of procrastination are ended. That lesson helped me the most—at the Academy and in my career.

The Academy also taught me that there's nothing more valuable than working hard. If you have a basic level of intelligence and you combine that with hard work, you can do anything. Every day you have the ability to get up and succeed or fail.

After graduation, Commander Denneny served in the Navy for 22 years, and did realize his dream of flying. A naval flight officer with over 3,200 hours in the F-14 and F/A-18, he commanded a squadron, earned a Distinguished Flying Cross and also served as a speechwriter and legislative assistant at the Pentagon. He now works for a major defense contractor and is running for the US House of Representatives.

This chapter has given you a glimpse of how the professors at the Naval Academy approach teaching and learning. The next chapter contains advice and observations in the professors' own words.

SIX
The Professors Speak About Academic Preparation

Almost all plebes are surprised by how much they struggle with their classes.

Vice Dean Michael Halbig remarked, "Kids who have been very bright in high school and, therefore, not pressed too hard by the high school system, will get a big shock here." The courses that cause the most problems vary from midshipman to midshipman, but the most often mentioned were calculus and chemistry.

Professors from the English, mathematics and chemistry departments were asked to give their opinions on why the plebes had trouble in their classes. They were also asked for advice on what candidates can do to better prepare themselves for their courses. Here is what they had to say.

READING, WRITING...

The first and most significant problem comes under the heading of poor reading and writing ability.

Said one professor who also is a naval officer: "Plebes come in here and have no idea how important it is for a naval officer to be a good writer. That is partly because they do not understand how the naval services really work. For example, they think everybody does everything in response to an order—that everything is just cut and dried—that a senior officer gives an order and it is passed down, adapted, then blindly obeyed. They are shocked when they realize how much give and take there is at each level of command.

"Most commanders seek input from the officers below them when they make their decisions. And when a junior officer comes up with an alternate approach or a different idea during an oral presentation, often he is told to 'put it in writing.'

"So it is very important to the career officer to have good writing skills. One never knows when a written proposal will be sent up through the chain of command. It is really out of one's hands then—it's too late to amplify a point; it must stand on its own. Also, it is possible for a brand new junior officer to write something that a senior officer thinks is a good idea. In that case the senior officer may use much of the junior officer's prose when he passes on the idea to the officers above him. That is a heady experience for a young officer the first time it happens. Needless to say, it also is good for the young officer's career."

Another professor made some of the same points while justifying the English Department's emphasis upon developing good writers. But he added, "I tell these kids that you have to become a good editor as well as a writer. As a junior officer you will have to write things for your superior—sometimes because he is lazy or because he is not confident of his own writing ability. Then you are in potential jeopardy because if you write something for him and he finds fault with it, this might cast a cloud over your other abilities and cause you to be misjudged. If you are careless enough to submit something with errors that he can discern, then you are leaving yourself wide open to criticism. We don't want someone taking those kinds of cheap shots at you; we want to teach you to write in such a way that you can avoid them. We want you to develop enough writing and editing ability so no writing assignment will make trouble for you."

Midshipmen are training to defend their country and fight its wars if needed, and to be effective they must be able to communicate in writing. That is why the professors hold them to such a high standard. What can a candidate do to become a better writer?

Said one professor: "If there is a creative writing course in your high school, take it. If one is not available, check into the availability of a night course in the local community adult education program. Those who do not have such opportunities can do other things. What is important is to do a lot of writing. Write letters—lots of them. Write your friends. Write your relatives."

> *Midshipmen are training to defend their country and and ... they must be able to communicate in writing.*

Said another: "Writing is like an athletic skill; the more you practice, the easier it becomes. But kids don't get a lot of practice in many high schools, so if they want to improve their writing, they will have to do things on their own. In that regard I think one of the best things they can do is to keep a daily journal. It doesn't have to be a soul-searching diary. It can be a factual account of one's activities with emphasis upon descriptive writing."

Since writing is so important, the Academy provides a writing center with tutors to help midshipmen work on papers. Said one of the professors who oversee the writing center, "A lot of students we get got A's in high school English. This is a different kind of writing—more critical thinking.

"The biggest problem is organizing their evidence, connecting it smoothly, making it flow coherently with a sense of a unified argument, and not just a bunch of isolated pieces of information. They tend to think the work is done once they have gathered the information and written a whole bunch of paragraphs. They don't realize that this is just the first step."

Midshipmen also have trouble doing research. Many will pull one book off a library shelf, or visit one web site of questionable credibility, and consider their research complete. If you have never written a paper that required extensive research from a number of different sources, spend some time with your high school librarian learning how.

Once you know how to gather a variety of sources, you must be able to organize what you read. Said one professor, "A problem I see is that plebes waste a lot of time when they are reading and gathering material for a paper. They should think as they read, and they should jot down their thoughts and ideas as they go along. This speeds up the organization process and helps them sort out ideas that can be implemented when they begin to outline their paper. It would help them if they would practice this in high school."

Many professors pointed out the connection between good readers and good writers, and the need to be a good reader to succeed academically at the Naval Academy.

Said one English professor, "A lot of the kids have not read much when they get here. And from my experience, after many years of teaching plebes, those who have the most trouble in our English classes are those who have read the least. Reading is a subliminal way to learn grammar and syntax. Unfortunately these kids, having been raised with television, have heard good English spoken, but they have not read much of it. Therefore, they can't reproduce it like they would if they were used to seeing the printed words."

They should think as they read, and they should jot down their thoughts and ideas as they go along.

What should you read? "I think the main thing we would like to see in midshipmen is not so much having read specific individual works, but having the habit of reading—of wanting to read and doing so whenever they get a chance."

Said another: "To prepare for this place I would advise any candidate to do a lot of reading. Ideally they should read some of the classics—any English teacher could give them a list of 8-10 titles that would give them good reading experiences. But if they won't do that," continued the professor, "there are other things they can do to help themselves. For example, I personally would recommend that they subscribe to a good, large-city newspaper during their senior year. Then they should get in the habit of reading it every day. Especially important is the editorial page, which is often a gold mine of good writing. Also, by reading the editorial writers every day, they will be knowledgeable of all the major issues of the times."

Still another said, "My advice to the candidate is to read more than you have ever read in your life and don't be too concerned with what. I think it's unrealistic to expect high school kids to read the classics—although it would be good for them. I would tell them to read anything in which they are interested, or anything that gives them pleasure. That way they at least will have some motivation to keep reading."

The English professors were not alone in stressing the importance of reading skills. Said a chemistry professor, "Another weakness is their reading ability. The reading vocabulary of the average chemistry textbook—the number of terms and concepts introduced in a short time—is one of the highest of any college subject. And, while many problems are done in math, the concepts on which they are based must be comprehended from the written word."

Said another professor: "The students who have the most trouble are those who do not know basic grammar. When they have written a bad sentence, for example, I might say, 'Let's break this sentence down and see which pronoun, who or whom, should be used. First, where is the noun?' Typically, that's where the trouble begins. We cannot even get into a discussion of the nominative or subjective cases because the kid cannot identify the noun. It's as bad as trying to diagnose car trouble when you get under the hood and don't know where the carburetor is or what it does."

What should a candidate do to correct such a deficiency?

"Get a handbook of grammar—there are many good ones out there," said a professor. "We use the Simon and Schuster handbook and it is very good. But get any handbook and go through it systematically. Do the exercises and when you stumble on something, ask yourself why you are having problems. Then get at the root of the problem or get an English teacher to help you.

"It wouldn't take most students long to review the basics of grammar and it would really help them to have this knowledge fresh on their minds when they arrive. Many have had good training but it was in the eighth or ninth grade. That is too long a lapse for many of them."

Another recommendation is for candidates to familiarize themselves with a spell checker and a grammar checker. The midshipmen all have computers with this software and they are expected to use it when they begin their first year English classes. It is rare to see a paper with a misspelled word because the students learn that they must do a spell check.

...AND ARITHMETIC

All midshipmen must take two years of mathematics. During plebe year they take two semesters of calculus. The second year they take a third semester of calculus and one semester of differential equations.

Each plebe is given a math placement test during Plebe Summer. This allows the math department to place the plebe in one of three different calculus courses, all covering the same material but at different rates. Each year, a few plebes are found to be mathematically deficient and must pass a special non-credit class in algebra and trigonometry before embarking on the two-year sequence of calculus and differential equations.

Good math skills will be expected.   USNA Photo Lab

Many plebes described calculus as their biggest academic headache. Why do many plebes have trouble with their math classes? The professors believe that their problems are not usually the result of the difficult concepts taught, but more often come from a weak foundation in basic algebra.

"I think most of them have trouble," said one professor, "because they can't do the algebra. I see it all the time—when they start working with algebraic fractions, for example. They get into trouble adding fractions, inverting fractions, dividing fractions; they tend to write down what they think is right and they just push on and don't stop—they waste a lot of time that way. And they do dumb things—they will add one over A, plus one over B, and put down one over A plus B. Those are the kinds of mistakes that just tear them apart."

"I agree," said another professor. "Many are deficient in algebraic skills all across the board. That is so frustrating because we don't teach algebra here—not in our calculus classes. It is very frustrating when they can't manipulate fractions or quadratic formulas, can't do simplifications and factoring or do not understand the properties of exponents. Those are just a few of the deficiencies that I see."

Why are students with good math backgrounds deficient in algebra?

Said one professor: "I think it is because of the attitude they had when they were taking the course in high school—that the algebra was something to be learned long enough for a test, not something that must be retained and built upon in later courses. Even when they are taught well, I think eleventh graders—typically that is the last year they take algebra—do not realize that they will need to use what they have learned. It's an attitude. They don't realize that they have to keep their learning intact."

The math professors were asked what candidates could do to come better prepared. One professor repeated the obvious: "Learn your algebra. Get good at it. Work especially hard applying algebra in word problems—that is the real test of whether one really understands it or not."

Said another professor: "Don't forget trigonometry either. Know and understand how to work with sines and cosines. I see kids hit trig and it becomes a real hurdle for them. When they have to work with sines and cosines, it becomes a psychological barrier and they think they can't get through it."

Said one math professor, "I see a change in the plebes coming in. Their algebra and geometry skills are degraded from what we saw in the past. Maybe it's because kids are taking algebra earlier than they used to. Maybe it's a maturity factor. Maybe they weren't ready for algebra at the time they took it. But, they definitely need a strong algebra background when they come in here."

And, just as with writing, good math skills will be expected across your academic classes. A chemistry professor explained, "Chemistry itself is not the problem at all. The primary problem is the lack of ability to apply algebra to word problems. They are used to memorizing facts and regurgitating them. When they have to analyze a problem, then set it up using an algebraic equation, they find themselves lost."

Said another chemistry professor, "Also, there are specific kinds of math knowledge that I see lacking in our chemistry students that could be mastered in high school. Our kids have trouble working with basic trigonometry functions, so learn those and feel comfortable using them. It would also help to understand natural logarithms, which they can do if they take calculus. Natural logarithms are introduced here in our calculus classes, of course, but it is done too late for when they are needed in chemistry. They are used when we get into kinetics and first-order rate laws.

"They should master simple algebra concepts. They should know how to apply the binomial theorem to problems. They should be comfortable working with base-ten logarithms. Also, they should really work at understanding graphing. The typical kid comes in here thinking of a graph as being like a pie chart—something like a graph that is used in business. Even though they have had it in their algebra courses, they do not think of a graph as x-y plots. They don't grasp the concept of plotting a function with a variable even though they have probably done it many times in their high school algebra."

LEARN TO UNDERSTAND

These comments all suggest that you must learn AND UNDERSTAND basic concepts, and be able to apply them, in order to succeed at the Naval Academy. The previous chapter discussed how to change your attitude toward learning so that you learn to understand, and learn for the long term. Many professors at the Naval Academy repeated this idea.

Said one math professor: "I think the problem is more in the way they learned the algebra. Many learn by rote memorization. They want to know how to manipulate the letters and numbers without doing too much thinking—without understanding how or why they can do the manipulating. Then, when they get here, they expect to use the same approach and it doesn't work. They have to apply their algebra and think their way through a problem. That is a new experience for many of them; a tough experience. That is why many have trouble with calculus."

A chemistry professor said, "I think these kids are preconditioned during Plebe Summer. In that program they have to memorize, memorize, memorize, day after day. Of course, they are smart and they figure out tricks that help them—they get good at memorizing after a while. But then they come to our chemistry classes and want to do the same thing. It seems like they are always looking for the magic trick that will allow them to solve chemistry problems, and, of course, there is no such thing. Except for a couple of chapters, rote memorization will not work with chemistry. They have to use reasoning."

Said another, "If I was giving advice to a young high school student, a freshman, for example, I would say take all the math that you can and do not look for the easy ways out. Take all the tough classes and never take a study hall. Push yourself and try to develop study habits that demand that you give a certain amount of attention to your classes every day, not just before tests. Most important, you must demand more of yourself than the high school does."

Learning without thinking – rote memorization – will not be enough to get good grades.
USNA Photo Lab

Said another: "I recommend that they change their attitude about their high school math. They think of it as a subject to itself, unrelated to chemistry or physics. They should think of it as something to be mastered so it can be used in other subjects."

A chemistry professor explained, "I encounter a large number of students who come to me and say, 'Sir, I read the assignment—I read it two or three times but I still failed the quiz.' It's because they read the assignment but didn't learn to solve the problems. Most got by with their intelligence in high school and didn't have to learn how to solve problems. My advice: learn to solve problems; that's the best preparation."

One final bit of advice came from the father of one of the chemistry professors who is an award-winning high school chemistry teacher. He cautioned against the passive, sit-and-get learning discussed in the previous chapter.

He said, "Students always have trouble with word problems. My advice is to tackle that deficiency head on. When you take high school chemistry, do the word problems on your own, before you go to class. Do them even if they are hard and require a lot of work. Take pride in going to class and watching how your fellow students have to be spoonfed—who have to have the method for solving the problems explained to them by the teacher. Of course, you won't be able to solve all the problems without some help. But develop an independent attitude—an attitude where you will get great satisfaction out of needing the teacher as little as possible. A kid with this kind of independent attitude will survive anyplace."

If you practice this approach in high school, your academic shock at the Naval Academy will have a much lower voltage.

DON'T FALL BEHIND

Almost all the professors interviewed mentioned the need for a firm mastery of the basics—a solid understanding of the foundational concepts of reading, writing, and math. Another piece of advice came up again and again. The advice: Do not allow yourself to get behind.

Said one professor: "I see it all the time. A plebe gets under pressure, often from the upperclassmen, then sloughs a homework assignment. Then he gets snowed in class but thinks he can dig himself out that evening. But then something else happens—more pressure, perhaps, then the inevitable happens. He gets behind.

"Don't let that happen. Every professor hands out a sheet during the first day of class. That sheet explains when the professor is available for EI [extra instruction]. Every plebe should use that EI time immediately when something is not understood. The problem is that the plebes are not used to classes where so many concepts are interrelated and built on each other. Therefore, they don't realize what kind of a jam they are getting themselves into when they get behind."

The midshipmen call the first-year chemistry course the "plebe killer." The professors who teach that course were asked if it deserved that reputation and, if so, why?

"There is no question that chemistry is a difficult course for most plebes," said one of the professors. "But it isn't because we set out to flunk all the plebes. It is because of a combination of problems, some related to the nature of the subject, but many related to other factors. Let me try to explain.

"First of all, chemistry is a class that demands a lot of daily attention. We go through 10 to 15 pages a day and that is a lot of material that must be absorbed. And unlike history and some other subjects, one cannot just wait until the night before a test and cram for several hours. That won't work and it takes the plebes time to realize that. Of course, by that time they are in trouble.

"Just keeping up on a daily basis is a problem because of all the other pressure that is on the plebes. If they were in a normal institution, they could spend more hours each day on their studies. But they can't do that here. Their time is limited and they are not efficient in the way they allocate it. Of course, most of them were never pushed in high school, so it takes them a while to adapt after they get here."

Writing assignments present a different time management problem. These assignments are usually handed out weeks in advance, but a plebe's attention tends to gravitate to the most urgent or threatening demands. Explained one English professor, "Having gone here, I know the pressure can really make you feel constrained to do only what is most immediate. A lot of times people don't feel as though they have the extra hour to spare because they have to work on a quiz and it's hard to have a longer term view."

Good writing, however, takes time and thought. "You don't produce your best work if you do it all the night before. If you do 10 or 15 minutes of work on the paper on Monday, and another 10 minutes on Tuesday, you get the ball rolling. If you just get a little bit written down, your subconscious kind of starts working on it. With writing assignments, you need a day or two from writing to come back and look at it with fresh eyes. I would encourage that, especially if one anticipates having a hard time with writing."

A professor from another department summed up the same advice with an expression that dates back to the days of the sailing ships. "A stern chase is a long chase," he said. "It is very difficult to catch up when you get behind. So the best advice is not to allow yourself to get behind in the first place."

The mental demands of the Naval Academy are enough to wear a plebe down, but add the physical demands and some find themselves completely overwhelmed. Physical preparation is the subject of the next chapter.

SEVEN
Physical Preparation

Do you like to push yourself physically? Do you like physical competition? Answer those questions as you decide whether the Naval Academy is for you or not.

If your answer is "no," and physical activity is something you dread, or something you do only when it is required, you should probably forget about going to the Naval Academy.

Why?

The Naval Academy is a physical place. Every day, the midshipmen are engaged in some activity that is physically competitive. Half-hearted participation is frowned upon, and the physically weak are in for a lot of special attention that they will not enjoy.

To understand why the Naval Academy places such a heavy emphasis on physical fitness, you must realize that the Navy expects its officers to remain trim and fit throughout their careers. They must perform the physical tasks required of their jobs, and they must also have the stamina to work long hours, sometimes in harsh conditions, and set an example for the men and women they lead. In fact, an overweight or out-of-condition officer can be dismissed—after suitable warning, of course.

The Marine Corps is even stricter about physical conditioning. Marine Corps officers take pride in their combat readiness and their ability to keep up with the youngest and best-conditioned recruits.

Most important, according to a physical education professor at the Academy, is a favorable attitude about physical activity. "If the attitude is there," says the professor, "everything else will fall in place. The midshipmen will do well here with the physical challenges. And, when they go to the fleet, they will stay in shape because they want to—not because they have to."

"On the other hand," continues the professor, "if the individual reading your book doesn't enjoy physical activity, I'll make a flat statement to that person: don't come to the Naval Academy. If you do, you will not enjoy it here. You'll always be forcing yourself to keep up and that's too heavy a burden to carry for very long."

A first classman put it another way. "Just as soon as they get here, I can tell by their faces if they're dragging. You know then that you can eat them for breakfast—you know they're going to have problems."

Let us assume that you answered "yes" to the questions at the beginning of the chapter. You do like competitive physical activity and you look forward to it. What then?

Do you enjoy pushing yourself physically? USNA Photo Lab

You should convince yourself that it is important to prepare yourself physically for the Academy. This should include endurance training as well as activities that develop strength.

START STRONG

What if you are not in good physical condition when you come to the Academy? Can you survive?

Mixed replies were given to those questions at the Academy. According to one PE professor, "If they can walk when they get here, they can survive."

Another PE professor said, "Don't scare prospective candidates by making them think they have to be in top physical condition when they get here. The important thing is for them to be in good enough shape so they don't get blisters or muscle strains. If that happens, they can get behind and find themselves in trouble."

The midshipmen were more persuasive with their comments. One said, "I went overboard getting in shape before I came and during the first few days it was almost a letdown because I expected it to be more difficult. But then I looked around and saw those who weren't in good condition. They were dragging and all the other pressures of Plebe Summer were getting to them while I was almost enjoying it. It was then I realized how glad I was that I had trained before I came. Definitely those who were not in shape suffered a lot more than I did."

Another midshipman restated the warning the physical education department gave about injuries: "The worst thing that can happen is for someone to get injured, like pull a muscle. Then you cannot participate; you get behind and you get left out. Come with your muscles in shape—make that a good strong recommendation."

Another reason for preparing physically has nothing to do with surviving the physical challenges. A first classman put it this way, "One of the best ways of attracting the attention of the first classmen during Plebe Summer is to be out of shape. It seems like those who are out of shape are always picked on more than the others. Also, those who are a little overweight seem to draw more than their share of attention. On the other hand, if a plebe looks sharp and is in good shape, I think the first classmen have a tendency to think, 'Well, that one looks squared away; we can leave him alone for awhile.' So my advice is to come here in top shape just so you won't catch as much flak from the upper classmen."

A third classman listening to the above comment added, "She's right, but I think what's important is to show energy, energy, energy—that's what the upper classmen respect. Show energy and you'll get their respect. Drag it and they'll stay on you and ride you. Lots of times I didn't know my rates, but I shouted the answers with energy and they left me alone."

Another third classman added, "That's really true, and those I felt sorry for were the overweight ones. Face it; if you're a slob, you're going to get picked on. I wouldn't want to come in here overweight. They make you lose the weight—we got weighed every week during Plebe Summer and they weigh you each semester during the year. But what a hassle trying to lose

Many midshipmen recommend being able to run three 7:30 miles with no strain.

USNA PHOTO LAB

weight with all the other pressure that you have the first year. That's just something else to worry about and you have more than enough already."

So what is the best advice?

Both the PE professors and the mids are correct. You probably can go to the Naval Academy without being in top condition and survive. Nothing is so difficult that most healthy young people with average strength cannot ultimately get through it after participating in the Academy physical conditioning program.

However, you probably do not want to set yourself up to do it the hard way. So remember these two points.

First, if you are in excellent shape when you arrive, Plebe Summer will be easier physically.

Second, if you can demonstrate excellent physical fitness, you are probably going to be harassed less than those who are out of shape.

HOW TO GET IN SHAPE

The Naval Academy has a recommended exercise routine for you to follow in preparation for Plebe Summer. You can find it on their website at www.usna.edu//PEScheds/workouts.htm. This workout provides a detailed regimen for improving your aerobic capacity, flexibility, and pushups and situps.

Because this workout directs you to run or swim or do some kind of aerobic training for a certain amount of time, it will not give you a sense of how well you are doing relative to what will be expected.[1] How can you tell if you are fit enough to keep up with the physical demands of Plebe Summer?

The midshipmen who were interviewed for this book offered more specific goals. They stressed that preparation should include running distances longer than just a mile or two. A general consensus of one group was that you should be able to run three 7:30 miles with no strain. One graduate recommends running four miles a day, and being in good enough shape so that those are "easy" miles.

Most intercollegiate athletes enjoy the physical aspects of Plebe Summer, because for them running and other physical tasks are familiar, comfortable, and relatively easy compared to the other demands they face each day. However, the midshipmen cautioned that "jock types" sometimes have trouble because they think they are in shape when they are not. Do not just assume that you will be able to keep up. Go for a run, time yourself, and see when you start getting tired.

Many midshipmen recommend using weight machines for developing strength. This is especially true for developing upper-body strength, which is where midshipmen are most likely to be deficient, according to members

---

1. The workout schedule advises you to run at a pace based on your PRT, or Physical Readiness Test, pace. The PRT includes a 1.5 mile run time of no more than 10:30 for men and 12:40 for women.

Not surprisingly, swimming is important at the Naval Academy.   USNA Photo Lab

of the physical education department. But if you do not have access to a gym, you can still work on your strength. You can install an inexpensive pull-up bar in a doorway, and you can do lots and lots of pushups.

Not surprisingly, swimming is an important activity at the Academy. You do not have to be a good swimmer when you arrive…but it helps. Those who are good swimmers may be able to validate a course and use that precious time for other purposes.

The poor swimmers have to keep working at it, and each year the demands are increased. Your second year, you will have to be able to jump off a ten meter tower, float for three minutes, and swim underwater 50 feet fully clothed. If you are worried about the swimming requirements, you can read more at www.usna.edu//PEScheds/pecurriculum.htm.

The bottom line is this: Prepare yourself physically. Be in excellent shape when you arrive at the Naval Academy because it will make your first year easier and give you one less thing to worry about.

EIGHT
Other Preparation

You cannot get into the Naval Academy just by being a good student—even with outstanding grades and SAT board scores. You have to offer more than that.

You must demonstrate that you have had experiences outside the classroom. You must prove that you have developed skills other than strict academic skills.

EXTRACURRICULAR ACTIVITIES = LEADERSHIP POTENTIAL

What kinds of experiences are necessary? And why?

In high school, you have many opportunities outside the classroom to use and develop your capabilities. Examples include team sports, clubs, student government, newspaper and yearbook staffs, drama, band, drill team, chorus and debate.

They also may include ECA outside of school such as Explorer and Eagle Scouts, church and community volunteer service, Civil Air Patrol, Junior ROTC, Sea Cadets, and fraternal organizations.

ECA are important for those who want to go to the Naval Academy because participation demonstrates the qualities that are valuable at the Naval Academy and in naval service. For example, a student who has played football or run on a cross-country team has experienced hardships, learned self-sacrifice and developed mental toughness. Also, such a student has learned the value of teamwork and has developed a competitive attitude.

Participation in ECA demonstrates that candidates are not selfish with their time—that they have a desire to serve. The desire to serve others is an essential part of a naval officer's makeup. Those who are self-centered and selfish with their time are better suited for other careers.

The ability to get along with people is another essential trait for a naval officer. When a candidate can demonstrate ECA leadership experience, that is an even better indicator of officer potential. To those who evaluate candidates, it is far better to have been the elected president of one club than to be simply a member of three. Likewise, it is better to have been a team captain, a newspaper editor or student council president than to have been just a member of those groups.

A student who has held leadership positions has learned something else that is considered valuable by those who evaluate candidates, a skill all successful midshipman must possess: time management.

At the Academy there is never enough time to do all the things that are supposed to be done. In order to survive, the midshipman has to

If possible, borrow a copy of Reef Points.   USNA PHOTO LAB

compromise and prioritize. Some things have to be left undone and others have to be done in their order of importance. Midshipmen have to find time for relaxation and recreation, without letting their play get in the way of their work. That is called time management.

High school students who take hard academic classes and hold ECA leadership positions have had to learn some of those time management skills. A candidate who is both a scholar and a leader is considered to be better prepared for the rigors of the Academy than one who has never been pressured for time.

In addition to ECA, work experiences also are considered important by some people who evaluate candidates. For example, several panelists who serve on congressional screening committees have flatly stated that they prefer candidates who have had real-world work experiences.

Why are work experiences considered so important?

You must realize that for most panelists their main goal is to evaluate the motivation and potential dedication of the candidates who come before them. Some panelists believe that students who have worked at summer jobs or at part-time jobs while attending school are more likely to have the kind of motivation and dedication that is needed to survive at the Academy.

Others see work experiences as just one more opportunity for the candidate to learn to manage time. And candidates who have to work to help support their family will impress the panel as someone who can handle responsibility.

Certainly, while being interviewed by a panel, if you are asked what you have done during your last two summer vacations, the interrogator is not likely to be impressed if you answer, "I spent my last two summers having fun."

Junior ROTC or any extracurricular activities with a military focus (such as Sea Cadets or Civil Air Patrol) are especially valuable. These ECA provide candidates with opportunities to learn about military culture and traditions, practice leadership, and gain exposure to people with experience serving in the military. Participation in JROTC also shows that you are seriously committed to serving in the military.

GET A HEAD START

Some other types of preparation for the Academy are not essential for getting admitted. However, there are things a candidate can do prior to enrollment that will make life at the Academy much easier.

The first concerns various kinds of naval knowledge, known as "rates." As soon as Plebe Summer begins, the new plebe is required to master seamanship terms, naval engineering terms, standard ship commands and a very long list of other facts. All of these are contained in a little book called *Reef Points*, which is issued to each plebe. If possible, find an upper-class midshipman or Academy graduate and borrow a copy of *Reef Points*. You can make it easier on yourself by memorizing, or at least familiarizing yourself with much of the material in that book.

If you cannot find a copy of *Reef Points*, you can still get a head start on your rates. Go online or to the library and learn about the Navy—its ships, rank structure, and history.

Plebes are also expected to read the daily newspaper and keep up with current events. It is recommended that you start this habit several months before going to the Academy. It will help you to have the background and perspective for what you will read about later.

All midshipmen learn the theory and techniques of sailing. If you can get a head start and learn the theory, you will have more time just to enjoy the sport.

Some midshipmen recommend you learn how to shine shoes. When learning that skill at the Academy, it may take as much as an hour to get your shoes shined to the satisfaction of the upperclassmen who will inspect you. It is better, say the mids, to solicit the help of a former military person to teach you to shine shoes to military standards before you go and while you have plenty of time. Then, in the time crunch of Plebe Summer, the chore can be reduced to a few minutes of skilled work.

SEE FOR YOURSELF

Another recommendation—one that is given enthusiastically by nearly everyone who knows anything about the Academy—is to make a personal visit and see for yourself what the Academy experience is all about. There are several good ways to go about this.

The best way is to participate in the Naval Academy Summer Seminar. You can apply on line in February of your junior year at www.usna.edu/Admissions/nass.htm. A Summer Seminar application also counts as a preliminary application to the Naval Academy (see Chapter 9).

Summer Seminar provides you with a taste of Naval Academy life, including academic, military, and physical training. You will participate in teambuilding exercises, and get a taste of life as a plebe. Summer Seminar participants also go to the Iwo Jima memorial in Washington, D.C., run through the obstacle course, and participate in a character development seminar. According to an officer from the admissions office, "The idea is to go away knowing whether this is the right place for you."

Summer seminar provides a taste of Academy life.   USNA PHOTO LAB

Participants receive room, board, and equipment for $300. They must also pay for their own travel to and from Annapolis. The program is very competitive, offering about 1,800 slots for 6,000 applicants. If you are selected for Summer Seminar, you automatically become a candidate, the first hurdle to receiving an appointment to the Academy. Historically about a third of Summer Seminar attendees receive and accept appointments to the Naval Academy.

How does one get selected for Summer Seminar? First, if you have taken the P-SAT and done well, there is a chance that you will be on the Academy mailing list and will receive information on how to apply. But, if you really want to attend, do not wait around to hear from the Academy. Go after it on your own by contacting the blue and gold officer in your region or visiting the admissions web site.

If you do not participate in Summer Seminar, the Naval Academy Visitors Center provides tours specifically for potential candidates. Admissions tours, which include a video and briefing on the admissions process, take place four times a day on weekdays and twice on Saturdays.

You can also participate in a sports camp. The Academy offers week-long camps in a wide variety of sports. While you will not experience Academy life directly, you will have the opportunity to see the yard up close, and perhaps interact with some midshipmen. If you attend a sports camp, you will have to pay the cost of registration and travel. More information is available at www.navysports.com.

Finally, you may have the opportunity to participate in a Candidate Visit Weekend. If you become a candidate, you will be invited for a Thursday through Saturday visit where you will be paired with a mid, live in Bancroft Hall, and go to classes. You will be responsible for travel expenses, while the Academy provides room and meals.

What if you cannot visit the Academy? You may not be able to take time away from your job or other activities. You may live too far away and be unable to afford the travel expenses. Will the fact that you have never visited Annapolis count against you in the admissions process?

Probably not. According to a blue and gold officer from Hawaii, those candidates who cannot visit compete just fine. If you live in Baltimore, less than an hour away from Annapolis, a nomination panel would be surprised if you never took the time to see the Academy up close. But if you live in Alaska, do all your other homework, and become as informed as you can about the Academy and the Navy...everyone will understand why you have not visited.

So far this book has described some of the challenges you will face if you go to the Naval Academy, tips for preparing yourself, and a chance to review your personal motivation for wanting to apply. Do you still think you want to be a midshipman? If so, read the next section very carefully. The next chapters describe how to navigate a complex and competitive admissions process that will eliminate about 90 percent of your competition.

HOW TO GET IN

NINE
Applying To The Academy: Getting Started

Getting into the Naval Academy is not an easy process. There are letters to write, forms to complete, a medical examination, a physical fitness test, letters of recommendation to solicit and perhaps several interviews. In addition, there are deadlines to be met and appointments to be kept.

If you are serious about going to the Academy, you should be happy that the process is so involved. Why? Because the complexity of the process helps eliminate some of your competition.

When faced with all the forms and letters, many students give up immediately. Others start the process but are careless, either with the forms, the deadlines or the appointments they make. They eliminate themselves. Every competitor who is eliminated helps your chances—if you are determined to do the process correctly.

And you must realize there is a lot of competition. Each year, about 11,000 people begin the application process. Out of the initial applicants there may be nearly 2,000 who complete the process, secure a nomination and are found fully qualified. Yet there are only about 1,300 openings each year!

In ski racing, the difference between the winner of a race and those who finish second, third and fourth may be just hundredths of a second. Much the same concept applies to competition among fully qualified Academy candidates.

Fractions of one point often separate those who get in and those who do not. But you should not be discouraged by this. You should look at it as good news because you can gain points in the admissions process IF you know what to do and what NOT to do.

So here is some advice on the first steps of the admissions process—advice from a variety of sources, including Academy officials, congressional staff members, blue and gold officers, high school counselors and midshipmen who retain vivid memories of their own experiences.

GETTING STARTED: THE SOONER THE BETTER

The first step is to determine if you are eligible for the Academy or will be eligible at some future date. Here are the requirements:
- Be at least 17 years old.
- Not yet have passed your 23rd birthday on July 1st of the year you will enter the Academy

- Be a U.S. citizen by the time you enter the Academy (international students authorized admission are exempt from the U.S. citizenship requirement)
- Be of high moral character
- Meet high leadership, academic, physical, and medical standards.
- Be unmarried, not pregnant, with no dependents (including dependent parents)

Your next step, if you think you can meet the above requirements, is to visit the Admissions web site, www.usna.edu/admissions. The web site contains the most up-to-date information on the admissions process, as well as general information on such things as the curriculum and types of majors that are available.

Note that you must complete a Preliminary Application as a first step. In the spring semester of your junior year, around the beginning of April, the Preliminary Application will be available for you to complete on line.

All those who are involved in the admissions procedure recommend that you START EARLY. For example, during your sophomore year you should ask your counselor for the dates when the Preliminary Scholastic Aptitude Test (PSAT).

During your junior year, take the regular SAT or ACT tests as soon as you can and repeat them if you can afford it. The Naval Academy will accept your BEST scores.[1] The LATEST you should take either the SAT or ACT for the first time is June following your junior year.

If you take them later, you will probably not have the scores back in time for the deadlines imposed by your nomination sources. Most Congressional offices require all applications to be complete in October or November of the year you are applying.

Work closely with your school counselor during all phases of the application process. Experienced counselors have usually been through the admissions process several times with other students. Some have visited the Academy on special orientation programs.

BLUE AND GOLD OFFICERS

Also, you should work closely with your blue and gold officer, or BGO. There are more than 2,000 BGOs in the U.S. who serve as Naval Academy representatives. Many are Reserve officers, although some are still on active duty, some are counselors or educators, and some are parents of midshipmen or graduates. Many are Naval Academy graduates themselves.

---

1. They will take your best verbal and math scores from different SATs. For example, if on the first try you get a 680 Verbal and a 650 Math score, and on the second try you get a 660 Verbal and a 670 Math, they will credit you with a 680 Verbal and 670 Math score for a total of 1350.

The BGO's job is to identify and counsel prospective Academy candidates. Many times they meet and counsel students who are in the ninth or eighth grade—or even younger students who think they might want to go to the Academy. BGOs will tell you that the sooner you can get together, the more they can do to help you prepare. Said one, "If I don't meet them until they are juniors, it's almost too late for me to help them. We have to start a lot earlier to make sure they're taking the right kind of courses and doing the right things" to be competitive.

BGOs also participate in the selection process. They evaluate each candidate in their district, usually after one or more interviews and after reviewing the candidate's written statements. Their evaluation is very important because their report tells the admissions board about your motivation, attitude, and potential.

How do you find your BGO? Your school counselor or JROTC instructor may know who he or she is. If not, call the Naval Academy Candidate Guidance Office at (410) 293-4361 to find out.

Then what? Telephone or write your BGO as soon as you consider going to the Academy. Often the BGO will try to arrange a get-acquainted meeting with you. He will answer your questions, discuss what an officer's life is like or, if you are more seriously interested, counsel you about preparation or admissions. Do not hesitate to contact your BGO even if you are still in junior high school.

The BGO's job is to identify and counsel prospective Academy candidates.

BGOs like to counsel students who still have plenty of time to prepare for the Academy. As one BGO explained, "If we can get to them when they're 8th or 9th graders, we can make sure they take the appropriate courses, and that they know about opportunities such as summer seminar and sports camps."

Realize that if your parents contact your BGO for you, the BGO will wonder who really wants you to go to the Academy—you or your parents. One BGO remembers a parent who called repeatedly on behalf of "Johnny," until the BGO asked in frustration, "Doesn't Johnny know how to use the phone?" Better to call the BGO yourself.

Before your first meeting with your BGO, learn as much as you can about the Academy. That way you can ask specific questions, which demonstrates that you are interested enough to have spent time investigating. BGOs know how much information is available on line. At the very least, make yourself very familiar with the admissions web site, including the on line version of the catalog. That will impress the BGO. Everyone in the admissions process expects you to do what you need to do with minimal help. Several BGOs said they watch how quickly candidates complete their paperwork to evaluate how motivated they are.

Your BGO will be very helpful in counseling you about the next step in the admissions process, which is to apply for a nomination. All candidates for the Academy MUST HAVE A NOMINATION before they can be offered an appointment. Obtaining a nomination is the subject of the next chapter.

ARE YOU QUALIFIED?

How does the Academy decide who is qualified and who is not? Your BGO will explain the whole process, and the web site has many of the details. But here is a brief summary. Each eligible candidate is evaluated on the following general criteria.

Are you medically qualified? The Naval Academy graduates officers to lead in the operational Navy and Marine Corps. They must be able to withstand the physical demands of a combat environment, and may be deployed in austere conditions where medical care is very limited. Poor eyesight, including color blindness, is a common reason for medical disqualification.

What if you are told you are not medically qualified? Is your dream of attending the Naval Academy over just like that? Many medical conditions that are disqualifying at the first look are often waiverable after further review. If you had some childhood disease or other condition that resulted in the initial "no" answer, but that condition does not affect your life now, you may still be able to attend. It is worth your trouble to request a medical waiver.

Other special programs, such as flight school, have more stringent medical requirements. Imperfect eyesight is the most common cause of disqualification from flight school. But if your eyesight is less than perfect, note that surgical procedures to correct nearsightedness may disqualify an individual from entry into the Academy. Admissions officials recommend you do not have corrective surgery before you arrive. Surgery, under the supervision of Navy doctors, may be an option later on.

The most important criterion for admission, other than physical qualification, is academic potential. This is determined by the candidate's grades, rank in class, college courses completed (if applicable) and SAT or ACT scores. In a recent Academy class, more than 80 percent of the midshipmen had graduated in the top 20 percent of their high school class. About 75 percent had SAT verbal scores over 600, and 87 percent had math scores over 600.[2]

Another important factor for admissions is the candidate's extracurricular activities, because they tell the admissions board about your

---

2. Or ACT scores over 26.

leadership potential and your ability to juggle multiple responsibilities. These include school activities such as athletics, clubs and student government and also community activities such as scouting, JROTC, Sea Cadets, and church activities. The admissions board is also interested in your summer and academic-year work experiences.[3] More points are awarded for leadership roles than for simple membership.

The final consideration is the BGO's assessment based on the interview. While his or her recommendation cannot help you overcome a weak record, they tip the scales in favor of someone who is on the border line. And perhaps more importantly, the BGO can flag you as someone not motivated or mature enough to succeed at the Naval Academy. As one BGO explained, "I can't get you in, but I can keep you out."

In all your meetings with the BGO, including formal interviews, he or she will be assessing certain of your qualities. How confident and mature are you? Do you communicate well? Do you display leadership qualities? Is there evidence of your ability to work with others? How interested are you in pursuing a military career? How much effort have you made on your own to learn about the Academy? These are the kinds of questions BGOs must ultimately answer when they write their evaluation.

COMMON ADMISSIONS MISTAKES

Many candidates make costly mistakes in the admissions process—mistakes that hurt their chances of getting into the Academy. Most of these are easily avoided. Here is how.

1. BE THOROUGH WITH ALL THINGS

"My pet peeve," said a congressional staffer, "is the candidate who leaves empty blanks in a form. Then, when I ask the person why, I get a dumb answer like, 'Oh, my coach is going to write a letter telling you all that stuff.'"

The above incident is one example of how candidates hurt themselves by not being thorough. Another is when the candidate says to his BGO after all his paperwork has been submitted, "Oh, I forgot to put down the summer job I had at Burger King between my sophomore and junior years." How do you think such carelessness might affect the BGO's rating of that candidate?

Before you even start the application process, create a file listing all your achievements. Organize them into categories such as academics, sports, community service, and clubs. Remember to include every job, activity, award and volunteer effort—student of the month, head of the charity clothing drive, team co-captain, or bus boy at the local restaurant. It

---

3. Candidates who have to work to supplement family income often have limited opportunity for club or sport involvement. The board understands this situation and will not penalize the candidate for their lack of extracurricular activities; the candidate is showing the ability to handle responsibility by holding a job and helping to care for his or her family.

all shows your ability to take on added responsibility and stand out above the average high school student.

It might feel like bragging, but you have to tell the admissions board why you are Naval Academy material. Do not rely on others to sell you— no one knows all you have accomplished as well as you, and no one else cares about your application as much.

2. BE NEAT

"Can you believe that I get letters and forms in here that are dirty or have coffee stains on them?" sighed a congressional staffer. That was one of many complaints heard from those who must deal with candidate forms and letters.

Neatness is a habit that WILL be learned if the candidate ever gets into the Academy. But those who deal with candidates generally look more highly at those who already demonstrate such habits. Give yourself every chance to be one of those who are thought of in that way.

Be neat. Be neat with your paperwork. And be neat with your appearance—neat hair, shoes, and clothes make an impression on everyone, especially those with a military background.

3. ALWAYS BE ON TIME OR, BETTER, BE EARLY

What is your opinion of the following three candidates? All three say they have a strong desire to go to the Academy. But one of them shows up ten minutes early for an interview, the other just exactly at the minute the interview is to start, and the third shows up five minutes late.

Are you likely to think that the first candidate, the one who showed up early, has the most desire? That is the way most evaluators think. So pay attention to deadlines. Get your paperwork in on time—if you cannot get it in early. Get to your appointments on time—if you cannot get to them early. NEVER BE LATE WITH ANYTHING IF YOU CAN HELP IT.

One BGO mentioned that nearly every November, he gets a call or an e-mail from a candidate asking about the congressional nomination process. The answer by that point is, "It's too late now." His advice: Pay close attention to all deadlines.

4. CHECK ALL GRAMMAR, PUNCTUATION AND SPELLING

Everyone will make mistakes when filling out forms or writing letters. The important thing is to CATCH those mistakes before they go out and tell the world that you use poor grammar, cannot punctuate, or cannot spell.

There is no reason for a candidate to submit forms or letters with mistakes. To prevent this from happening, do two things.

First, write out the answers on a separate sheet of paper or hit "Print Screen" to create a hard copy of on-line forms. Second, ask your counselor,

English teacher or some other qualified person to read your forms and letters to make sure there are no mistakes in grammar, punctuation or spelling. Just checking them yourself is not enough.

When you are filling out forms on line, it is very easy to hit "submit" before you have thoroughly reviewed all your responses. But there is too much at stake for you to take a chance. Review every entry for accuracy. Remember, there is nothing wrong with asking for help. After all, professional writers do the same thing. They submit their work to editors who check what they have written before it ends up in print and possibly embarrasses them.

5. ALWAYS REMEMBER, YOU, AND NOT YOUR PARENTS, ARE APPLYING TO THE ACADEMY

Consider this situation: A BGO shows up to interview Johnny at his house, and Johnny's father, who served for twenty years in the Navy, does all the talking and asks all the questions while Johnny looks at his shoes. Then Johnny's mother appears more interested than Johnny in how to fill out the on-line application or get a congressional nomination.

Maybe Johnny's mother and father, not Johnny, think he should go to the Academy.

Parents can provide wonderful support for candidates during the admissions process, and later if the candidate becomes a midshipman. But there is a big difference between support and ACTIVE INVOLVEMENT.

Everyone participating in the admissions process is deeply wary of parents who appear to hover like a helicopter over their son or daughter's candidacy. The tragedies of midshipmen who were pushed into the Academy by overzealous parents are well known. Every person who evaluates a candidate will be looking for that kind of parent over-involvement and SCREEN OUT that candidate.

As a seasoned BGO explained, "During every interview, I speak with the candidate one on one and ask if they really want to go. If not, I tell them, 'I can take care of that.' I use the interview write up [to convey their lack of motivation to the admissions board]. There are lots of ways to become an officer in the Navy or the Marine Corps; the Academy is just the hardest one."

So, take charge of your own admissions requirements. Do not rely on your parents to do the work for you or let the process get out of your control. Make all calls YOURSELF. Look upon each call you must make not as a chore, but as another opportunity to sell yourself. If your parents insist on helping, ask them to read Chapter 23. It is written just for them.

6. APPLY TO OTHER ACADEMIES AND ROTC

You might think it odd that applying to other schools would make help you get into the Naval Academy. But remember, the BGO and the congressional nomination panels are interested in why you want to attend the Naval Academy.

They are looking for young men and women who want to serve their country. If you are truly committed to that goal, it makes sense that you would pursue every possible path, including other service academies and ROTC programs at civilian colleges. Why would they believe in the motivation of a candidate who has made no effort to come up with an alternate plan for becoming an officer?

A BGO explained, "If I have to tell a kid to apply to ROTC, I'm not going to rank him very high. Why do you want to go to the Naval Academy? I need to hear about service to country, so if you are serious about serving, you should look at all the options. I believe I'm recruiting for the country, not just the Naval Academy."

Another BGO warned candidates to be cautious about saying that the Naval Academy is not their first choice among service academies. If you are not 100 percent sure that West Point or Air Force is your first choice, you may make a better impression with your BGO if you simply say that you are applying to other academies. Also, you may change your mind about which academy you prefer as the process goes on. However, if you are certain that Navy is your first or only choice, "Be honest about your preferences."

Regardless, make sure you have a reasonable back-up plan. Applying to other schools shows initiative and drive, and that you think ahead and are mature enough to realize that life does not always turn out as you would like. These are all traits that will serve you well if you do get into the Academy.

If you follow all these tips, you will make a positive impression on your blue and gold officer. You will also have the right frame of mind for embarking on the process of getting a nomination. The nomination is extremely important, because you cannot get an appointment without one— which is why it is the subject of the next three chapters.

TEN
The Second Step: Getting The Nomination

The spring of your junior year is when you officially begin the application process by filling out your Preliminary Application. It is also a good time to begin your quest for a nomination.

The procedure for getting a nomination is much more involved than the application process. In seeking a nomination you should probably make separate applications to at least four different nomination sources. Your four primary sources are the two U.S. Senators from your state, the U.S. Representative from your congressional district and the U.S. Vice President. In this book, U.S. Senators and U.S. Representatives will be called "congressmen" and their nominations will be called "congressional nominations."

You may also be eligible for a number of other nominations if you fit one of these categories:

- Children of active duty or retired military
- Children of deceased or disabled veterans
- Children of Medal of Honor recipients
- Active duty, guard and reserve enlisted personnel
- ROTC and JROTC midshipmen and cadets

The best way to find out if you are eligible for one of these additional nominations is to talk to your blue and gold officer.

The simplest of all the applications is the one to the Vice President. This nomination is also the hardest to get since only one or two are available each year for the whole United States. A sample letter is available on the Academy admissions web site, and more information is available by clicking the "Appointments" button on www.whitehouse.gov/vicepresident.

Getting a congressional nomination can be a lot more complicated because of the paperwork required. Also, many congressmen require that candidates go before a panel to be interviewed and evaluated.

Many states now hold annual Service Academy Information Days, where staffers from the congressional offices, blue and gold officers, parents clubs, midshipmen, and graduates make themselves available in one location to talk to prospective candidates. They will answer questions and give you resources and advice on the admissions process. Your school counselor, blue and gold officer, or congressional staffer can tell you if these opportunities exist in your state.

But what about politics? Do your parents have to have political "pull" for you to obtain a congressional nomination? Many people believe that to be true. Some believe that your parents have to belong to the same political party as the congressman. Others believe that your parents or relatives have to have helped in the congressman's campaign or contributed money to it.

Years ago some of those beliefs may have been true—service academy nominations were sometimes awarded as political favors. However, according to hundreds who have been interviewed for the books in this candidate series, the role of politics is relatively unimportant now. Congressmen do not want to waste their constituents' tax dollars paying for the wrong candidate to attend the Academy. They want to make sure the candidates with the best records and the best chance for success receive nominations.

NOMINATION MATH

There are a total of 535 congressmen—435 representatives and 100 senators. Each has a quota of five cadets or midshipmen who can be at each service academy at any given time. Thus, each year there is usually at least one upcoming vacancy because at least one of the five will probably be graduating. For each vacancy, the congressman can make ten nominations.

Do not let all those numbers confuse you. Just remember that for each vacancy, the congressman is entitled to submit a list of ten nominees from his state or district.

There are three ways the congressman can list those ten nominees when he or she submits the list.

By far the most common method is to make what is called a competitive list. By this method the congressman gives all the names on the list equal ranking. By doing it this way the congressman is telling the Admissions Office, "I have screened the candidates in my state/district and here are the ten who I think are the best. Now it is up to you to decide which candidates should be offered an appointment."

The second method is the principal/alternate method. By this method the congressman picks one nominee to get a principal nomination. This principal nominee, if fully qualified, must be offered an appointment to the Academy first, before any of the alternates on the list can be appointed. And if any of the alternates, which are ranked in sequence—first alternate, second alternate, third alternate, etc.—are appointed, they must be appointed according to their ranking if they are fully qualified.

The third method, which is the principal/competitive method, is a combination of the previous two. The congressman makes one nominee the principal nominee, but the nine alternates are competitive. The Academy can then decide who, if any, should be appointed from the list of alternates.

Admissions officials will pick one nominee from the congressman's list, either the principal nominee or the most qualified nominee if it is a competitive list. That nominee will be offered an appointment. If he or she accepts the appointment, that person is the one who will count against the congressman's quota of five who can be at the Academy at any one time.

However, the Academy usually offers appointments to others who are on the congressman's list of ten. Those who accept are not charged against the congressman's quota. So, even though each congressman has a theoretical quota of five who can be at the Academy at any one time, it is not unusual for one congressman to actually have more than 10 and sometimes as high as 20 or more at a service academy at any one time.

And for you, the candidate, that is good news. It means that even though your three congressmen might only have three vacancies the year you apply, your chances of getting an appointment are greatly increased because of all the alternates who are also offered appointments. Three congressmen with a combined quota of three vacancies could easily end up with 10-15 of their nominees being offered appointments.

Much depends upon the qualifications of the alternates. For example, on Congressman A's list of 10 nominees there might be only one who is highly qualified and in that case only the one might be offered an appointment.

But on Congressman B's list there might be five who are much more highly qualified than the nine who were left on the list of Congressman A. Therefore, Congressman B might have five of his nominees offered appointments.

Now let us turn to politics again. Suppose a senator or congressman did pay back a political favor and give some young person a nomination. In most cases the list is competitive, so perhaps one name on the list would be there because of politics whereas the other nine are there on the basis of their own merits. Since the list is competitive, which nominees are going to be offered appointments?

Answer: The nominees the Academy believes to be the best qualified. Therefore, if you manage to get yourself on such a list, you do not have to worry about competition from another nominee unless that nominee is better qualified than you. And if the person is better qualified than you, that person would have gotten a nomination without the political favor.

So, if you or your parents are worried about politics being a part of the nomination process, you are better off to forget it. You will be much better off concentrating on what you must do to earn your place on one of those three lists of nominees.

GETTING STARTED ON THE CONGRESSIONAL NOMINATION

The first thing you must do is contact the three congressional offices— the offices of your two U.S. Senators and your U.S. Representative. If your blue and gold officer has not already armed you with this information, go to www.house.gov and www.senate.gov. If you do not know the names of your congressmen, just click on your state and the site will lead you to the correct contact information.

Then call each congressman's regional office—use the one closest to where you live—and ask for the name of the "staffer" who handles the service academy nomination process. Most of the time the staffer who does that is in a regional office, not in Washington, D.C.

When you get the staffer on the phone, tell that person you want to apply for a nomination to a service academy—you do not have to specify which one. The staffer will ask you some basic questions such as your age, address, and year of graduation.

In addition, there is a good chance you will be asked to write a letter formally requesting to be considered as a candidate for a nomination—or a letter explaining why you want to go to a service academy. Why would a staffer ask for such a letter? Why not just send out the congressman's packet of application forms and instructions? There are at least two reasons.

First, there is a common problem of young people calling up saying they want to apply for a nomination just on a whim. They think, "Hey, going to the Naval Academy sounds like a neat idea. Why not go for it?" Senators in heavily populated states will get well over a thousand people who are serious about getting a nomination. Requiring a letter is one way of eliminating those who are not really serious.

You are being evaluated every time you interact with someone involved in the admissions process.

The second reason why staffers may want a letter requires a little more explanation. Staffers know there are parents out there who, for economic reasons or to enhance their own prestige, want their sons and daughters to go to a service academy. Some push their sons and daughters openly—often it is a plea to get a free education and save money.

But more often the pressure is subtle—so subtle in fact, that the young people are not really aware they are being pressured. They are manipulated in such a way that they have begun to think that going to a service academy is their own idea.

In either case, it is the sons and daughters who are going to suffer because the record of those types surviving at any service academy is absolutely disastrous—previous chapters have already discussed this trap. The academies are very tough: tough academically, tough physically and tough mentally. Those who have very strong self-motivation are the ones who survive. Those who have been manipulated into going to an academy by their parents normally do not. So, just as blue and gold officers do, congressional staffers try to use the admissions process to eliminate those who are not really motivated.

DO IT YOURSELF

Staffers say they get many calls from parents wanting to know what a son or daughter has to do to get a nomination. And from the staffers' comments about such calls, the parent might as well be waving a red warning flag in front of the staffer's face. When a parent calls, the immediate question in the mind of the staffer is, "I wonder if this is a parent who is pushing a kid into applying for an academy?"

So, many staffers do what they can to flush out overzealous parents—and to protect young people from the psychological trauma of eventual failure. When a parent calls about a nomination, some staffers will politely ask the parent to have the son or daughter call, saying—to be diplomatic—that there are a number of questions he or she would like to ask the candidate before sending out the congressman's information packet.

Of course, another way to make an end run around an overzealous parent is to require a letter from the candidate. If the candidate is poorly motivated, he or she can procrastinate writing a letter and in this way thwart the parental pressure. At least that is what the staffer is hoping.[1]

Staffers see another warning flag when parents do the calling for you. Succeeding at the Naval Academy requires maturity, initiative, commitment, and self-motivation. If you need your parents to get you through the application process, you probably do not have the traits required to succeed in the high-stress environment of the Naval Academy.

Remember that you are being evaluated every time you interact with someone involved with the nomination or admissions process, not just when the application is read or the formal interview is taking place. Take advantage of every opportunity to make yourself known and present yourself well.

ATTENTION TO DETAIL STARTS NOW

After you have called the staffers and perhaps sent in letters that were required, you will receive three separate application packets—one from each congressman.

It is very important that you follow the instructions in each packet exactly, because each congressman has his or her own philosophy and his or her own way of awarding nominations. Almost nothing makes a staffer so angry as when a candidate takes the information from another congressman's packet and duplicates it. Do not give the staffer the impression that you are not serious enough to pay attention to the smallest details.

---

1. A field representative said that he always makes it a point to tell candidates, "Hey, if this is something you really don't want to do but you don't want to hurt your parents, just leave something out of the application that you send to the academy. The academy probably won't call or write you about it and you won't hurt your parents because they will never know that you sabotaged the application."

So take each packet and keep your materials for each congressman in three separate files. Also, make copies of everything that you submit, marking on each one of them the submission date, and keep those copies in the three separate files. That way you have a record of everything. You will know what has been sent to whom, and when it was sent. If you would consider going to West Point, the Air Force Academy, or the Merchant Marine Academy, be sure to mention that. Give your order of preference; you may receive nominations to more than one academy.

Almost every congressman (and also the Admissions Office) will require that you solicit letters of recommendation. Here are some dos and don'ts that will help you get the best possible recommendations.

Do not just walk up to a person from whom you would like to have a letter and ask, "Mr. ___, I'm applying for; will you write a letter of recommendation for me?"

Instead, tell the person you want the letter from that you are thinking of applying to the Naval Academy and you are wondering what that person thinks about the idea. This way you get a chance to feel out the person to see if he or she thinks it is a good idea. Perhaps that person will hedge a bit and wonder if you have what it takes for such a challenge. Or, that person might have a strong anti-military bias and feel that you would be wasting your ability going to a service academy. However, another person might be very enthusiastic and think your idea is wonderful.

The competition is tough... You certainly do not want any half-hearted letters of recommendation in your file.

Which person do you want writing a letter of recommendation for you—the person who is hedging or the person who is enthusiastic about you? The latter, of course. That is the reason for feeling out each person first. Find out if the person is solidly behind you, then ask for the letter of recommendation. The competition is tough enough already. You certainly do not want any half-hearted letters of recommendation in your file.

When a person has agreed to write a letter for you, you should give that person three things:

(1) A self-addressed, stamped envelope for each letter that has to be submitted. Typically, each person will be writing letters to all three congressman and perhaps the Admissions Office, too.

(2) A written deadline that is at least two weeks before the actual deadline. Why? Because the person you ask may be very busy and might forget the deadline or forget to write the letter. Then there are those who are procrastinators—they keep putting it off. (According to congressional staffers, high school principals are the worst procrastinators of all.) By giving an early deadline you can check

to see if the letters have arrived and if they have not, you will have time to prod the letter-writers and still make the real deadline.

(3) A print out of the file you made recording all of your school and out-of-school activities, awards, elected offices, test scores, community work, part time jobs—and anything else a person writing a letter needs to know about you. Why? Because that person wants to write the best letter possible (you hope) and to do that he or she needs to know all the facts about you. It would be the rare teacher, counselor or principal who knows all of your achievements, even though you may have been in the same school together for four years. So do not take any chances. Give them plenty of ammunition so they can fire their best shots.

Then what?

There is much more advice that could be given, but it will perhaps mean more to you if it is given in the words of some of the 40-odd staffers who were interviewed by the authors. Their comments are the subject of the next chapter.

ELEVEN
Tips From Congressional Staffers

The role of the congressional staffer varies considerably from office to office.

At one extreme are the staffers who, by themselves, review all applications, interview all candidates and then make up the lists of nominees that they present to their congressmen, who usually rubber-stamp the list. Staffers like this are very powerful. They know it—and they will let you know it.

At the other extreme are the staffers who only handle the paperwork while an outside panel or the congressman reviews the applications and makes up the lists of nominees. Staffers like this are strictly paper-shufflers and have no input whatsoever on who does or does not receive a nomination.

Most staffers have a role somewhere in between those two extremes. Many screen the applications and use their own judgment—often supported by objective criteria specified by the congressman—on who should be nominated. Also they may sit on panels and help interview candidates, or they may take the ratings of panelists and use them to make lists of nominees for the congressman.

And while most of the latter types will try to pass themselves off to candidates and parents as mere paper-shufflers, do not believe it. It is reasonably safe to say that most staffers have at least some power to decide who does and who does not get a nomination. Most of them have been in this role for years; they have seen it all, and will not hesitate to decide whether you are Academy material or not. So be careful. When you are dealing with a staffer, it is prudent to assume that this is the person who is going to decide whether or not you get a nomination.

Now let us hear from the staffers themselves. Dozens of them were interviewed. Many told of one or more visits to the academies. Most expressed strong feelings about the country's need for high-quality military officers. And most indicated that they were doing everything they could to recruit and nominate the best candidates from their district or state.

SHOW YOUR COMMITMENT

Staffers have some frustrating problems with their candidates. One of these problems is the way some candidates procrastinate.

Said a staffer from Arkansas: "They [the candidates] put things off till the last minute and don't realize that I have responsibilities other than handling academy nominations. We have deadlines to meet, too. When a kid pushes me because he has procrastinated, it is going to affect his overall rating."

And a staffer from Washington State: "Some call you up the night before the deadline and say, 'I don't have my pictures yet,' or 'I can't take my SAT until next week.' Or they bring in their letters, transcript, etc. the day of the review and want me to put the file together. That doesn't reflect good organizational ability. That doesn't show dedication. We are going to be skeptical about such candidates. Will they follow through if they get to an academy? They didn't follow through with us when they were told in September what we would need by the first of December. How are kids like this ever going to make it at one of the academies?"

And a staffer from Iowa: "They should be more timely because I won't even consider anybody who doesn't get their paperwork in on time. How could they be a successful at an academy if they can't do that?"

Another frustrating problem for staffers is candidates who do not follow up and check on their files. They point out that numerous things can be missing from a file. For example, SAT scores could be missing because they were sent to Winslow, AR instead of Winslow, AZ—mistakes like that occur all the time.

Another common problem is that high schools, including those with excellent reputations, often leave essential information like class standing off transcripts that they send out.

"...the ability to follow instructions has to be at the top of the list when it comes to considering candidates for an academy."

"The problem [with not following up]," said a staffer from Arkansas, "is that few of these kids really understand how important it is to stay in contact with us. Often there is something missing from their files and before the cut-off date we used to write or call and tell them about it. Now, because of the volume of applications, we just can't do that. Now we just use what is here and some kids will get hurt simply because they don't follow up to see if anything is missing. Of course, in our instructions we tell them to do that. So if they fail to do it they are not following instructions and in my book the ability to follow instructions has to be at the top of the list when it comes to considering candidates for an academy."

And a staffer from Texas: "What bothers me is that these youngsters put their trust in the people they ask for letters [of recommendation], then they fail in not double-checking with me...and I'm not perfect—something could get lost here or in the mail. But to be quite honest, they are supposed to be mature enough to handle four tough years at an academy...we can't coddle them. I've seen what happens at those academies. I know what these kids are fixing to get into. If they can't get their act together for a few pieces of paper, what are they going to do when they get up there and report to the academies for basic training—how are they going to handle that?"

Candidates who do follow up with staffers almost always leave a good impression.

Said a staffer from Iowa: "We do everything in our Washington, D.C. office, and since I never see any of the kids, it is the contact through the telephone and their letters that we use to help judge them. And one thing we know is that these kids hate to write letters. Therefore, it is really impressive when we get a nice letter or two from a kid checking on his file. Of course, we like them to call, too, but when a kid goes to all the trouble to write a letter, you feel that that kid is really motivated and wants to go [to an academy]."

And a staffer from California: "The bottom line is how much do they really want this thing? If they come to me for an application and for the interview and if that is all, they don't want it. I want them to bug me, to bother me. If they touch base with me, that shows that they want this thing. I remember one young man from a Catholic boys' school where 99 percent of the graduates go to college. Three kids from that school had applied but only one came in to see me on a regular basis. West Point, his first choice, was not interested in him but one day he mentioned that he was also interested in Navy. Right away I got on the phone and called them. I asked if there was any chance for him to get a Naval Academy Foundation scholarship. Now, this year, he is a firstie [senior] and has a nomination to go on to graduate school and get his master's. The point is, he came in and I worked for him. Sometimes the academies call me and say, 'What do you think about this guy or that guy?' I'll tell them, 'This guy, yes, because he comes in and follows up—that other guy hasn't shown up so I don't know.'"

Said a staffer from Iowa: "We had a kid this year who badly wanted to go to the Naval Academy but his grades were not high enough to make it. He came in for an interview—just to see what other options might be available. The kid looked like an outstanding candidate so later I just picked up the phone and called them and said, 'If you can't take this kid directly into the Academy, will you please consider him for the prep school?' He ended up there and I know that it will help him."

A staffer who is on your side can really help you.

MORE IS NOT BETTER

Some staffers are bothered by things that other staffers do not seem to mind. An example is when a candidate disobeys instructions and submits more letters of recommendation than were requested. Here are some typical comments:

A staffer from Ohio: "It is really dumb when they submit a whole pile of letters—one had sixteen sent; another had twenty and I was about to kill him! I have to write and acknowledge all of them! We ask for just three and we specify that they should be from persons who know them, who have been in contact with them, know their abilities, know their leadership potential, truly know them as a person. It is not going to impress me that the Honorable Joe Schmo who knew the kid's parents in the forties writes a letter—I'm not even going to put those kinds of letters in the file—I have to make four sets [for the panel who will interview the candidates] and I'm not going to duplicate all of those. Then there are those from the neighbor and Aunt Tillie that tell what a fine person the boy is. I won't put those letters in. Our panel who reviews them doesn't care if your Aunt Tillie says you are a sweetheart and you mow her lawn. They are looking for leaders, not sweethearts."

And said an Arizona staffer: "You know what I do when the applicant doesn't follow instructions and has a whole batch of letters sent? I take the first three letters, no matter who they are from, and I duplicate them. Those are the only letters that the committee sees and the candidate might be hurt if those aren't the best letters. I'm sorry, but that's the way it is. If the candidates can't follow the simple instructions that we give them, how can they expect to get by [at an academy].

Some staffers also complained about candidates who try to puff their applications with extraneous material.

Said another Ohio staffer: "We are not impressed with attendance awards or a twenty-page essay on why you will make a good cadet or midshipman. We don't request that and we don't want it. We had one kid who put a whole book together—that and fifty cents would get him a cup of coffee."

PARENTS: KEEP OUT

Parents who want to help their sons and daughters with the nomination process are also a problem—not for staffers—their ability to handle all kinds of people diplomatically is a mandatory skill for their job. Unfortunately, the overzealous parent is a problem for those whom they most want to help: their own son or daughter.

Said a staffer from Arkansas: "I've been at this business for 14 years and if there is one thing I have learned, it is to be leery when parents get involved. When mama and daddy are involved, we immediately get worried. We learned the hard way that those kids [who go because their parents want it] don't last at the academies. It is the ones who do it on their own who survive and graduate. My advice to candidates is to not let their parents run the show—we want to know what the applicant wants or desires—we don't want mama and daddy wanting to put their kids in the academy."

Said a staffer from Nevada: "Leadership is what it is all about and they should be able to demonstrate leadership from the moment they start the application. I am not impressed by the child if his parents call me and say, 'What else does Johnny need for his files?' I always wonder what Johnny can do."

Said another staffer from Ohio: "We get a lot of calls from parents and I'm not saying that is wrong. But, if young people are serious about going to an academy, they should make the calls themselves. They should learn how to do this on their own and they should call again if they have questions. This shows maturity and I will remember a kid like that."

Still another staffer from Ohio was more adamant: "I get these calls all the time. 'My Freddie is interested in going to a service academy' and I say, 'That's fine but let us hear from Freddie.' I guess the initial call is fine, but from then on it should be the kid who calls. And to the kid I would say, 'If you don't have the wherewithal to do things for yourself, you don't belong in an academy.'"

It is not always possible for a candidate to keep his or her parents out of the process. But give it your best effort.

When telephone calls need to be made, you make them.

If you need to visit the congressman's regional office, let a parent drive you if that is necessary, but go inside by yourself.

And by all means, when you go for an interview, do not let your parents accompany you past the door. An Arizona staffer told of one mother who became angry and created a scene because she could not accompany her son into an interview. "Can you believe that?" said the staffer. "How could we dare send a kid like that to an academy when mom is not going to be there to hold his hand?"

THE DO LIST

Most of the staffers' comments you have read have been negative in tone. But they were selected for that purpose because you should know the kinds of things that staffers do not like.

You should also know what kinds of things impress staffers. Thus, it is appropriate to conclude this chapter with a list of these things—some of which have already been mentioned or implied.

Staffers are impressed with candidates who:

- Call them early—say, during the spring of their junior year.
- Are polite and use good manners when speaking over the telephone or when they present themselves in person.
- Are dressed neatly and are well groomed.
- Have done their homework—who know what is on the admissions web site, who have talked with midshipmen and graduates and who have either visited the Academy or read about it.
- Get their paperwork in early.
- Follow up to see if anything is missing from their applications.

Perhaps most of all, they are impressed by candidates who write them letters. So, if you really want a staffer to remember you, write when you apply for your application. Write follow-up letters to let the staffer know what letters of recommendation to expect and, later, to make sure all of them arrived. Then write again before the deadline to make sure everything is complete in your file. Also, as a courtesy, if the staffer has done some favor for you or if you get a nomination, write a thank-you letter.

The staffers will appreciate the letters because they know how much you hated to write them. (Most of the staffers probably hate to write letters, too.) So, they will get the unwritten message in your letters which says: "Please pay special attention to me. I am not just one of your average candidates. I am much more serious and much more determined than the others—that is why I didn't just pick up the phone and call you like the others will do. I wrote those letters because I want you to know how much I want to go to the Naval Academy."

Said a staffer from Colorado, "I love this part of my job. I get to work with some really great kids." Be one of those really great kids.

TWELVE
Interviews: Advice From Those Who Conduct Them

When you apply to the Naval Academy you will almost certainly be interviewed by a blue and gold officer.

Often this interview is conducted in your home so the BGO can also evaluate your parents' attitude. He or she wants to know how strongly your parents are supporting your application. Midshipmen do better at the Academy when they have strong parental support. The representative also will be looking for warning signs that your parents have pushed you into applying for the Naval Academy. Do not expect a high recommendation unless you can convince the representative that going to the Academy is your idea.

The BGO's evaluation of your aptitude and attitude bears considerable weight in the overall admissions package. Ideally, you have interacted with your BGO many times over the past year or more. You know each other fairly well. Do not let this familiarity fool you—your BGO is evaluating you every step of the way. The interview is simply the most formal part of that process.

In addition to the interview with the BGO, you also may be interviewed by staffers or panelists appointed by one or more of the three congressmen to which you will apply for a nomination. (It is rare for congressmen themselves to interview candidates.)

In the case of the congressional interviews it is important that you go into them well prepared.

Your first concern should be with the kinds of questions that will be asked. Surprisingly, after interviewing more than 80 staffers and panelists, it appears that most candidates are asked about the same questions. Also there was a great deal of agreement among those queried on the kinds of answers that are rated good and bad by the panelists.

THE QUESTIONS

Your interview may be as short as 15 minutes or as long as an hour. As one staffer put it, "The purpose of the interview is to evaluate the candidate's preparation and motivation. We're trying to decide whether they are ready for that kind of commitment."

Remember, your record must stand on its own—your grades and test scores and extracurricular activities must be competitive. That is not what the interviewers are trying to evaluate. They are trying to assess whether you have the right attitude to succeed at a service academy. Following is a list of the questions that you are most likely to be asked. After each question are comments about good and bad answers.

WHY DO YOU WANT TO GO TO A SERVICE ACADEMY?

This question is almost certain to be asked. And many panelists said that even though the question is anticipated by most candidates, it is still the one that is most difficult for them to answer.

What panelists want to hear is how you personally feel about going to an academy. They want you to talk about your background, your interests and your goals. They want you to explain how a service academy will fit in with the goals that you have set for yourself. "Personalize your answer," was a statement heard over and over from panelists.

Said an attorney from Pennsylvania: "Part of the problem is that their answers are so predictable. They'll say, 'It is something I have wanted since I was a child.' That doesn't tell me why—it just says that I want it. Or they will say, 'I have read about it somewhere and I've always wanted to do that.' That isn't any more helpful.

"Another predictable but useless reply is, 'I think it would be a challenge.' That doesn't tell me anything, either. I think they have to dig deeper for the answer to this question. They should relate their answer to their own personality—they should personalize it a little more—they have to talk about their goals and ambitions. They have to express their feelings to the extent that they are telling something about themselves. It is these personal kinds of answers that are impressive."

Said another attorney from Pennsylvania: "I like to hear things that indicate a strong motivation and commitment. I like to hear them talk about the Academy and tell what they like about it—what they observed if they went there for a visit...things that show a depth of knowledge, things that show they have made an effort to learn about it.

"I am also impressed when I hear things like, 'It has always been my dream to have a military career because ...,' or 'I know myself well enough to know that I like a disciplined environment,' or 'One of my favorite things to do is to read about battles and wars,' or 'I have grown up hearing my father, a retired officer, and my uncle who spent 30 years in the Marine Corps, telling about their experiences. I liked those stories and I would like the opportunity to experience some of the kinds of things they experienced'—those are the statements that show motivation on the part of the kid; they show that the kid knows what he is getting into. They are personal and you know that they aren't rote, pat answers—that the kid is not just giving a canned response to the question."

Panelists do not want to hear such comments as: "I want to go to get a great education." A great education is available at lots of colleges and universities.

Nor do they want to hear: "I want to go because my parents cannot afford to send me to college and this is the way for me to get a free education." The panelists who object strongly to this kind of answer point out that the Academy really is not free; a great amount of work is required to get through four years and, in addition, the graduate has to pay the government back by serving at least five years on active duty.

What panelists are really trying to determine is whether or not you really want to serve in the Navy or Marine Corps. That is the sole purpose of the Academy's existence; it is there to prepare a select group of naval officers to serve their nation in times of peace and war.

Does that mean that you have to convince the panel that you intend to remain in the military and make it a 20- or 30-year career?

Some panelists would, indeed, like to hear that kind of declaration. But a majority said they were skeptical of 17- and 18-year olds making such statements. Typical was a university professor from Pennsylvania: "He can say, 'I'm thinking about a military career, but I don't know for sure that is what I'll be doing [in the future].' That's okay, but anybody who tells me at eighteen that he knows he's going to be a professional soldier, that's malarkey. He has to be a lot more mature than the kids at the university where I'm teaching because they're never that sure about their future."

WHAT ARE YOU GOING TO DO IF YOU DON'T GET IN?

The real wording of this questions should be: "How serious are you about wanting a military career?"

If you are serious, the panel would expect you to say that the Naval Academy is your first choice, but you would accept an appointment to another service academy. They would expect that you have also applied for an ROTC scholarship. Or that you plan on attending a college with an ROTC unit so you can get the military experience and a year's college which will help you when you apply again next year.

If you do not have a contingency plan, the panel is likely to think that you have only a shallow desire to go to the Academy. Consequently, do not expect high marks with an answer like, "Oh, I think I'll just go to Ponderosa College and study engineering."

One Air Force cadet said this question helped him overcome a not-so-competitive GPA (he had good SAT scores, sports, and extracurricular activities): "I told them that if they didn't give me a nomination this year, I'd be back every year until I was too old. I think that convinced them how badly I wanted it, and to take a chance on me."

SUPPOSE YOU WENT TO THE ACADEMY AND LATER CAUGHT YOUR BEST FRIEND CHEATING. COULD YOU TURN IN YOUR FRIEND?

Some version of this question is asked to see how well you have researched the subject of the Honor Concept. The thinking of the panel is that a highly motivated candidate would know about that Honor Concept and would already have thought about some of the consequences of living with it. So this question is just another one aimed to measure your motivation. (For a discussion of the Honor Concept see Chapter 22.)

WHAT MAKES YOU THINK YOU CAN STAND THE STRESS?

This question is asked so you will talk about yourself. The panel wants to hear about the difficult, stressful situations you have encountered in your lifetime. Perhaps those were on the football field with a tough coach who yelled at you all the time. If so, describe the coach's actions and how you handled the criticism.

But there are other possibilities you might discuss. For example, if your parents are divorced and you suffered in some way in the aftermath, do not be afraid to describe how you coped with the problem.

Basically the panel wants to see if you have had any experience coping with stress. They do not want to hear answers like, "Oh, I'm pretty tough; I can handle it," or "I just know I can do it."

The key to answering this question successfully is to talk freely about yourself and give specific examples that show you have some experience with stressful situations.

WHO IS YOUR HERO?

This is a favorite question of some panelists so you should be ready for it. But with whomever you mention, you should also be ready to explain why you selected that person. Of course, your rationale will give the panel more insight into your beliefs and attitudes.

One word of caution. Before going into the interview it would be prudent to check out the political bias of the congressman. A liberal, anti-military congressman may select panelists with that same philosophy. Consequently, they might not think so highly of a choice like Douglas MacArthur or George Patton. On the other hand, a conservative congressman might have the same kind of panel that would grimace at the mention of an anti-war activist or your favorite rapper whom the panel is not likely to know or appreciate.

DO YOU HAVE A GIRLFRIEND/BOYFRIEND?

Some panelists do not like this question and think it unfairly invades the candidate's privacy. However, enough panelists mentioned it that you should be prepared to discuss the matter.

Those who ask the question are trying to see how a girlfriend or boyfriend relationship might affect your future success at the Academy. With all the other pressure on the first year midshipman, sometimes the pleading of a lovesick girlfriend or boyfriend is enough to weaken the resolve of the midshipman to where he or she will drop out. If you do have a strong relationship, be prepared to explain how you are going to be able to essentially abandon it for the next four years.

HOW DO YOU THINK THE UNITED STATES SHOULD DEAL WITH NUCLEAR PROLIFERATION IN IRAN?

Many panels will ask a current events question like the one above. Some panelists believe that academy candidates should be a cut above the average good student and be aware of world events. However, those panelists are probably in the minority.

According to most panelists who were interviewed, current events questions are asked primarily so the panel can see how candidates handle themselves with such a question. In other words, they think that most candidates will not know much about the question that was asked. But, will the candidate fluster or try to bluff his way through an answer? Or will the candidate have the poise and confidence to look the panelists in the eye and say, "I'm sorry, but I can't answer that. I have been so busy the past two weeks I haven't even picked up a newspaper or a news magazine."

It might also help if candidates would explain that they are aware that knowledge of current events is required by plebes at the Academy. But then be prepared for this question: "If you are too busy now to keep up with current events, how are you ever going to do it at the Academy when the pressure is much, much greater?"

WHAT ARE YOUR STRONGEST AND WEAKEST POINTS?

This is a common question designed, not so the panel can pick at your weaknesses, but to get you to talk about yourself.

Show confidence when you talk about your strongest points. Many panelists say that young people are often too shy when talking about themselves. Try to remember that one of the things the panel is doing is evaluating your potential ability as a naval officer. And a leader cannot be shy. On the contrary such a leader must project a strong image. So do not hesitate with the panel. They asked you to talk about your strengths so this will probably be your best opportunity during the interview to sell yourself.[1]

Be cautious when discussing your weak points. The panel does not want to hear about your sins or mistakes. Mainly they want to know what traits you are working to improve upon. For example, do you procrastinate like most people? If so, admit it, but also explain what you have done recently to try to overcome that weakness. Do you keep a messy room? If so, describe how you are trying to change so you will be ready for the

---

1. One panelist chided one of the authors about this comment, saying that a candidate came before him boasting of his achievements. He cautioned: "Sell yourself, but use humility. Don't come across as boastful." Remember, they have seen your record.

orderliness at the Academy. Do you have a quick temper? This is a more serious weakness, so be ready to explain how you are learning to control it.

HOW ARE YOU PREPARING PHYSICALLY?

The Naval Academy is a very physical place and most panelists know it. Therefore, you should be prepared to discuss a specific physical conditioning program that you plan to follow. If you are familiar with and participating in the Academy's recommended physical preparation plan, even better.

You are not likely to get good marks for an answer like, "Oh, I played football; I'm in good shape."

HOW HAVE YOU HANDLED FAILURE?

It is very difficult for some young people—particularly high achievers who are good candidates—to handle failure. To be sure, some high achievers have never experienced failure.

However, if a panelist asks that question, it is probably because he or she knows that failure at the Academy is inevitable. Not major failure, of course, but failure in small things is purposely induced by the upperclassmen.

So think about this question before you go before a panel. If you have not experienced failure, you should present an attitude that says, "If I fail and I have done my best, then I can't do anything else about it. But the important thing about me is that if you keep knocking me down I will keep getting up. Temporary failures are not important to me. I am not the kind of person who gives up when things are going bad. I am not a quitter."

HOW ARE YOU, A BIG, AGGRESSIVE, MALE ATHLETE, GOING TO HANDLE IT IF YOUR FIRST SQUAD LEADER IS A FEMALE AND SHE DECIDES TO PICK ON YOU? OR, YOU ARE A FEMALE, SO HOW ARE YOU GOING TO HANDLE A MALE SQUAD LEADER WHO IS BIASED AGAINST WOMEN AND IS DETERMINED TO MAKE YOU CRY, OR QUIT AND GO HOME?

Such questions may be asked by panelists who want to know if you have thought about some of the gender issues that often arise in our imperfect society. Perhaps you do not know how you might react, but you should at least think about the question so you can have an intelligent answer ready. Also, you should realize that the panelist who asks such a question probably has strong feelings about gender issues.

HOW TO PREPARE

So much for the typical questions. The next thing you should know about the interviews is how to prepare for them.

The most important thing you can do is ARRANGE A PRACTICE INTERVIEW. This may sound silly to some candidates and in fact one Air Force cadet said, when the practice interview was mentioned in a discussion, "What kid is going to go out and arrange something like that?"

The fact is, most candidates discover that they do significantly better in their second interview than they did in their first one. They give better answers to the questions. And they are more poised and confident.

Another fact is that you are reading this book because you want to get an edge on your competition. So try to remember what the cadet said and realize that he is right. Most of your competitors will not take the trouble to arrange a practice interview. So do what they will not do and get ahead of them!

Some of the best people to conduct a practice interview are military officers from any branch of the service. They can be located in almost any community or neighborhood and most would be very willing to give you a good workout—especially retired officers who have plenty of free time. Your BGO should also work with you. Not only will she be pleased to do it, but it is almost guaranteed that she will be impressed with your determination.

> *Most candidates discover that they do significantly better in their second interview than they did in their first one.*

I have been telling you that your parents should be hands off in the application process; however, they may be a big help preparing you for the interview process. The congressional interviews are not so different from many job interviews, so your mom or dad—or a family friend—can give you tips and help you practice, even if they have no military experience. Whom you go to for help matters less than making sure you practice before your interview.

As soon as you know when your congressional interviews are to be held, begin making specific plans for them.

For example, plan what you are going to wear well ahead of time so your clothes can be ready. As for what you should wear, most panelists were in agreement.

Most panelists believe that men should wear slacks, a dress shirt and tie. Many suggested that a sport coat should also be worn, however most felt that a candidate should not go out and buy something just for an interview. Several said they would just as soon see a young man in a nice sweater as a coat.

Several panelists mentioned shoes—some with negative comments about old dirty "sneakers" and leather shoes that were scuffed and unshined. The best advice is to wear well shined leather shoes if you have them. But if you do not, at least wear the newest athletic shoes that you have.

There was mixed advice about female dress, whether or not a dress or skirt is preferable to slacks. Most who commented on the matter did agree female candidates should not come dressed like they were going to a party. Go especially easy on frills, jewelry, makeup and high heels. Said a woman panelist from Nebraska, "I'll never forget one girl who came in teetering on three-inch high heels; the panel was not impressed."

While discussing clothing that candidates should wear, almost every panelist gave examples of bad taste that they could remember, such as color mismatches of ties and socks. So get some help in coordinating colors if you are in doubt about your judgment.

Others mentioned poor grooming—things like dirty fingernails and unwashed or uncombed hair. Several panelists laughed about some candidates who come in jeans, T-shirt, without socks or in a sweat suit. One staffer, laughing and shaking her head, remembered a candidate who came in shorts and sandals.

A retired general and graduate of West Point from Washington State perhaps summed up the matter the best. After discussing his belief that young men should appear in a coat and tie if they can, he said: "[These kids] are looking at a very significant event in their lives. That little session could change the next thirty-five years of their lives. A lot of the kids come in, first of all, not fully appreciating that, and certainly not showing much deference to the critical juncture where they find themselves."

The candidate should also plan ahead to make sure to be on time. If transportation looks like it might be a problem, plan ahead. Ask for help from your counselor or your BGO. Said one staffer, "Map the route ahead of time. Read the letter informing you of your interview very carefully. We've had candidates lose their letter, come at the wrong time, even come to our office when we were using a different location for the interviews. Read the letter closely!"

And by all means, telephone the congressional staffer should an emergency arise and you will be late for the interview or miss it altogether. Make sure your reason stands up to scrutiny. As the staffer explained, "We conduct about 125 interviews each year. When someone calls to reschedule for a dumb reason, it makes us wonder about their commitment." They realize you are involved in many activities—all serious candidates are. But if you can't rearrange your schedule to make this important interview, it had better be for a very impressive reason.

PRESENT YOUR BEST SELF

Now the planning is over. You are sitting in the congressman's outer office with many other candidates, waiting. And you are nervous. But you look around and see only one or two who look like you feel. But the others...they look so calm! Seeing these others looking so confident may suddenly cause your self-image to fade. You may even begin doubting whether or not you should be competing in their league. And you may ask yourself: Wouldn't it be better just to ease out of the room and forget about the whole thing?

Not if you really believe you have what it takes to be a leader. You can believe that everyone waiting with you is just as nervous as you are.

Leaders must have the ability to control their fears and make those around them believe that they are full of confidence. And if those who are waiting with you for an interview do, indeed, convince you that they are confident, give them an "A" for leadership potential. They are probably as nervous as you are, only they are controlling it and projecting another image.

So, make up your mind that you, too, are going to take control and project a confident image. That is what the panelists will be looking for. Said a rough-talking, retired colonel from Georgia, "[The interview] is a test. Part of the challenge is to keep from being flustered. You get a guy who goes all to pieces and wets his pants—you don't want him leading a platoon in combat and creating a panic."

Leaders must have the ability to control their fears and make those around them believe that they are full of confidence.

What else can you do while you are waiting? Rather than rehearsing possible answers to questions in your mind, you are probably better off trying to keep your mind uncluttered so you can give fresh, thoughtful, original answers to the questions when you get before the panel. Several panelists mentioned candidates who appeared to have all their answers memorized, then gave them with robot-like speeches.

Many panelists also complained about candidates who give brief answers to questions. "To get anything out of some of them, you almost have to drag it out," was a typical comment. While you are waiting, try to remember that the panel is waiting to hear what you are going to say. They want to do very little of the talking. So convince yourself that when they start asking questions you are not just going to give an answer—you are going to discuss the question with them.

Also program your mind so you are ready to discuss yourself. Every question they ask will be of a personal nature to some degree. Project your personality into that discussion.

One further thing you can do while waiting is to ask the receptionist or staffer for a list of the names of the panel. You might not be able to memorize all of them, but you should at least know the name of the chairman. Later, it will be impressive if you can reply to Mr. Williams or Mrs. Johnson when you only heard their names once during the introduction.

Now the time has finally come; it is your turn to go in and meet the panel. Usually the staffer will come out to the waiting area and escort you into the room with the panel. Then you will be introduced, typically to the chairman first; then to the other panelists.

Who will sit on the panel? It varies widely from congressman to congressman. They may be ex-military officers, community leaders, or parents. There may be only two or half a dozen. They all bring their own experiences and values to the interview, as well as guidance from the congressman as to what he or she is looking for in a service academy candidate.

If it seems appropriate and natural, shake hands with the chairman and, perhaps, with the others as well. And if you do that, shake hands with a firm grip. Many people harbor very negative feelings about any person who gives them a limp handshake.

You will be given a chair in front of the panel and it is important that you sit erect. Of course, you will not be expected to sit as erect as you would a year later should you make it into the Academy. But panelists often criticized the posture of candidates, especially those who slumped badly.

Panelists were also critical of those who cannot control their hands. Excessive wringing of the hands was mentioned several times, as was nervous movement. Probably the best advice is to put your hands in your lap or the arms of the chair and use them only for your natural gestures.

Candidates who expressed themselves well and who used good grammar were commended.

Another thing that bothered panelists was the use of current high school slang, and the excessive use of "you knows," "umms" and "likes." Candidates who expressed themselves well and who used good grammar were commended. Panelists also commented favorably about candidates who exhibited good manners and who used respectful terms like "sir" and "ma'am."

Some panelists believe that candidates should maintain eye contact throughout the interview. The strongest statement came from a panelist in Arizona. She said, "That's the single, most important thing that you can tell a kid who is going before a panel. Have him make eye contact and keep it. Now I don't mean that he is to look at my hairline or at my chin or at my nose. I want the candidate looking at my eyes! I watch for this with each candidate. The ones who are insecure and lack confidence don't do it—at least that is my impression. Those who have poise and confidence in themselves do. And which do I want to send to a service academy? No way am I going to vote for a kid who doesn't have confidence in himself, because he'll never make it."

You can also demonstrate confidence by hesitating after one of the panelists asks you a question. The natural reaction, if you are tense, is to blurt out answers as fast as possible. Fight that tendency. Pause and think for a few seconds before you reply. Of course, that requires poise on your part. But outward poise is one of the best indicators of inner confidence.

Panelists also have complained that candidates often either do not listen to the questions that are asked or that they ignore them. "Either way, he makes a bad mistake," said a panel chairman. "The candidates who consistently get the highest ratings are those who answer the questions precisely."

How do you give an answer that is not too brief or too rambling? One Admissions Liaison Officer (the Air Force counterpart to the BGO) gives the following tip for formulating your answers: "I like the STAR method—it stands for Situation or Task, Action, and Result." This simple technique keeps the candidate from giving short yes or no answers that do not fully answer the question. For example, if you are asked about your weaknesses or your ability to handle failure, you could describe the Situation or Task you had trouble with, then what Action you took to improve yourself, and the Result of that action. When you do your practice interview, get comfortable with this or a similar technique for answering.

> *"The candidates who consistently get the highest ratings are those who answer the questions precisely."*

At the end of the interview the candidate is usually asked if he or she has any questions of the panel. Typically, say the panelists, the candidates are surprised and often they think they should ask something. They often ask, "When am I going to know something?" which is a question that is better asked of the staffer before or after the interview.

If you know that one of the panelists is a service academy graduate or veteran, you could ask a question about their service, such as what they liked best about serving in the military. If you do not have a specific question in mind, several panelists suggested that the candidate should use the time offered to say something like: "I really don't have a question, but there are a couple of things you didn't ask me which I think are important for you to consider. Would you mind if I just took a couple of minutes to go over them?"

Remember that panelists are human. In the course of one or two days of interviews they will sometimes forget to ask things that are important. So, during the interview, keep in mind the things you have not been asked—especially those things, when brought out, that might make a difference in your evaluation. Then use the time at the end of the interview to point out those things.

Now the interview is over. The chairman will probably stand up, and perhaps the other panelists, too. If it seems natural, shake hands again. But for sure, thank the panelists for giving you the opportunity to meet with them. Also, make it a point to thank the staffer, too.

PRACTICE, PRACTICE, PRACTICE!

This chapter is nearly over and the author can breathe a sigh of relief, having relayed to you every important bit of advice that came from all the panelists and staffers.

But you, the candidate, cannot relax. You still have the interviews to face. And probably you are trying to juggle all the important do's and don'ts in your mind:

Do use good English

Do give complete answers, but ...

Don't ramble

Don't wring your hands

Don't slump in the chair

Don't use high school slang or too many "you knows"

Do look the panelists in the eye

Do use good manners

Etc., etc., etc,.

All of that together is enough to put anybody's mind into overload, especially when you have to go into a room with strangers for the first time.

And what to do about that? Perhaps the advice in the following story might help.

The original author of this book received a telephone call from a candidate in Kentucky whose father is an old friend. The candidate had used the raw manuscript of an earlier edition of this book to guide his own candidacy. He called with the news that he had just received his appointment. That was wonderful news, of course, and, in the discussion that followed, the young man was asked what advice helped him the most.

"There is no doubt about that," the young man replied. "The recommendation you made to do a practice interview is the best advice in that manuscript. Be sure and put that in the book."

The author replied: "Should I say anything more about the practice interview—something that would persuade others to do it?"

"Yes, tell them that it helped tremendously, and I mean tremendously!"

That conversation relates directly to the problem of the candidate trying to keep all the do's and don'ts in mind as the first interview is impending. And the best advice for the candidate is: DO NOT LET THE FIRST INTERVIEW YOU DO BE THE ONE THAT COUNTS.

Arrange one or more practice interviews. And use them to practice the do's and practice avoiding the don'ts!

THIRTEEN
Alternate Routes To The Academy

You have submitted all the paperwork required by the Naval Academy. You completed your nomination interviews. And now you wait, and wait.

Weeks pass. Then you start getting bad news. You did not receive a nomination from your representative and senators. Or perhaps you got a nomination, but then you got a letter saying that you did not get an appointment.

Now what?

Is your dream of attending the Naval Academy over? Are you sure you will never be a midshipman or a graduate of the Naval Academy?

If you are ready to give up already, perhaps the Academy was not for you in the first place. The Academy is not for quitters; it is for those who have the ability to face failure, pick themselves up, and figure out how to succeed the next time.

This chapter is directed at those with that kind of determination. If you fail to get in the first time you apply, ask yourself a few hard questions. Am I really qualified for the Naval Academy? If not, can I become qualified in the future? If you can honestly say yes, and you truly want to go to the Naval Academy, do not give up yet!

Here is why: In each entering class, more than 300 of those appointed do not come in right out of high school. Roughly a quarter of new plebes enter the Academy by alternate routes. Many of them faced rejection the first time they applied. If you are determined, an alternate route may work for you as well.

So, what should you do next?

If you did not get a nomination, call one or more of the congressional staffers who have your file. Explain that you have no intention of giving up—that you want to apply again next year. Then ask the staffer if he or she would please look over your file and make recommendations on what you can do to make yourself a better candidate. Realize, of course, that the staffer probably cannot do this immediately while you are on the telephone. So, with your request, also ask when it would be convenient for you to call back. This will give the staffer time to review your case and to think of advice that would be most helpful.

If you received a nomination but not an appointment, there are two people you should contact. One is your BGO. The other is someone from the Candidate Guidance Office at the Naval Academy (their phone number is 410-293-4361). Try to convince both of your determination to do whatever you have to do to get accepted for the next class. Then, as with the congressional staffers, give them time to review your application before you call them again. Also, you may receive a letter from the Admissions Office at several points in the process, providing you feedback on how to become more competitive.

While you are consulting with those who will be discussing your weaknesses or deficiencies, be very careful not to get defensive about yourself. Just listen to what they are telling you, and even if you think they are wrong, thank them for their efforts.

After the consultations, the next step is to evaluate what you have heard. Then you should develop a plan of action based upon your options.

You may end up like one young man who received a rejection letter. He realized that his leadership experience and SAT scores were not very competitive. During the spring of his senior year in high school, he was selected captain of his lacrosse team, got good grades, and got his SAT scores up. By that point, however, it was too late to go to the Naval Academy that summer. So the young man went to a good state university and reapplied. He is now a midshipman.

HOW TO BECOME MORE COMPETITIVE

One of the most common problems of unsuccessful candidates is an academic deficiency—demonstrated by a low grade point average or low test scores: SAT, ACT, or a combination of both. If this is your problem, you must demonstrate as soon as possible that you are capable of academic success at the Naval Academy.

How?

Get into a college as soon as you can. And take hard courses. If you prepared for it in high school, take calculus. Take English. And take chemistry. And work as hard as you can. Do more than you are assigned. Get as many A's as you can.

Also, take the SAT and ACT as many times as you can—remember, it is your highest score that counts.

In addition to your college classes you should also consider taking a specialized course designed to help you increase your SAT and ACT scores. Ask your high school or college counselor about local programs. Another option is to check your Yellow Pages under "Tutoring" or check for resources on line.

What kind of college should you attend?

A general recommendation would be to go to the best college you can afford and the best college that will admit you. Even better would be a college that has an ROTC (Reserve Officer Training Corps) unit that will accept you.

Ideally you should try to get into a Naval ROTC program. However, if this is not possible, do not hesitate to get into an Army or Air Force unit—

you are seeking an opportunity to prove yourself to military officers. The branch of service is of minor importance.

One midshipman reported success with this approach: "I just didn't get in the first time, so I went to Penn State and ROTC. It was a great way to prepare to get in here."

Perhaps your problem is not an academic deficiency. Perhaps you were not involved in many extracurricular activities while in high school. Perhaps those who evaluated your application felt that you were too "bookwormish" to make a good midshipman. If so, what can you do?

First, go on to college and do what has already been recommended. But get active in things other than academics. If you are in ROTC, get active and try to become a leader in whatever other clubs the unit sponsors that interests you. As one admissions officer at West Point said, "Get in and get dirty...and prove yourself."

ROTC midshipmen and cadets can compete for a special category of nomination. But even more important, being successful in ROTC will demonstrate your commitment to becoming an officer, and your ability to handle military and academic challenges at the same time.

Get involved in student government, the school newspaper, dramatics, intramural sports, clubs, or whatever else interests you. And strive for leadership positions.

Do not worry that you cannot be elected president of a club as a freshman. Do what you can. Volunteer for committees and take as much responsibility as the organization will give you. There are always opportunities. For example, few organizations will deny an eager freshman the opportunity to lead a clean-up committee.

And remember what you are seeking. You are seeking leadership experience. Also you are seeking leadership credentials that you can cite on your next application.

JOIN THE FORCE

What if you cannot afford college? You can enlist in the Navy or Marine Corps—the active force, or the Navy or Marine Corps Reserve— with the goal of earning one of the appointments given enlisted members each year.

You should realize that this option is much more risky than the college option. With the college option you can go on and get your degree, then perhaps get an officer's commission. But if you enlist, you might never get to be an officer. You might join for three or four years, not be admitted to the Academy, and end your enlistment without any college credit.

If you do decide to join the Navy or Marine Corps, here is some advice that has been handed down from others who have entered the Academy from that route.

First, you must excel at everything you do in order to earn good recommendations from your supervising officers. In boot camp, try to be the outstanding trainee. In whatever technical training program you enter after that, strive to be at the top of your class both in academics and in military qualities. Later, when you are given your active-duty assignment, try to be the best Sailor or Marine you know how to be.

In addition, make sure you have a copy of the regulation that explains the academy application procedure. It is not uncommon for personnel to know very little about the procedure. So do not depend upon someone else to tell you how to apply.

Let your supervising non-commissioned officers (NCOs) and officers know that your goal is to attend the Naval Academy. Those supervisors may give you responsibilities that will allow you to prove that you have leadership potential.

A word of caution: Some of your peers or immediate supervisors may not understand why you want to go to the Academy. They may even try to talk you out of pursuing an appointment. Why? They may feel you are betraying the enlisted force by seeking an officer's commission. Or they may resent you for taking a valuable asset (you: a hard-working, well-trained young troop) away from the unit. You will have to resolve to stay committed to your goals, and look past this kind of short-sightedness to pursue them.

While you work through the process, remember that you still have opportunities to improve your academic ability. Enlisted personnel can subscribe to a number of college-level correspondence courses. Also, most bases have off-duty college classes available that you may be able to take.

Few go directly from the Navy or Marine Corps into the Academy. Most spend a year at the Naval Academy Preparatory School, which is located in Newport, Rhode Island. The purpose of NAPS is to bring potential mids "up to speed" in math, English, physics, chemistry and information technology. Military and athletic training is also included, but it is not as rigorous as at the Academy itself.

PREP SCHOOLS

Prep schools are designed for promising candidates who are not quite ready to enter an academy. Often these are candidates who have demonstrated leadership potential, but who are slightly deficient academically. Many are recruited athletes or enlisted personnel.

You cannot apply directly to NAPS. Your application to the Naval Academy serves that purpose. The admission board will offer Prep School appointments to certain promising candidates who do not get appointments.

Candidates typically react in one of two ways when they are offered the prep school option. One candidate says, "Wow, that's a great opportunity. Where do I sign?"

Attending the prep school gives you a head start academically and militarily.

NAVAL ACADEMY PREP SCHOOL

The other candidate says, "What! You expect me to waste a year of my life in a prep school? You have to be kidding. I would rather forget about the whole thing and just go on to a college and take ROTC."

Before you react either way, you should think about some of the advantages of the Prep School option. First, it will give you a chance to strengthen your background in the subjects that are most difficult for first-year midshipmen. More than one graduate emphasized that the Prep School will lessen the academic shock you feel plebe year.

Second, and perhaps more important, the instructors will see to it that you learn how to study. Not knowing how to study is the biggest problem of first-year midshipmen who enter the Academy right out of high school.

Third, you will have one more year of maturity before you start the rigorous schedule of a plebe. That year of maturity will help you adapt to the many stresses of that first year. You will also be over the pain of homesickness, a malaise that creates problems for many who leave home for the first time.

Fourth, you will learn a great deal about military training. You will know how to shine your shoes and put your room in inspection order, and you will learn some of the military knowledge and culture that most plebes first encounter on Induction Day. This knowledge will give you more time to focus on your studies, and the opportunity to establish yourself as a leader among your Academy classmates. Every mid interviewed who had gone to NAPS said the year spent at Prep School made the military demands of plebe year much easier.

NAPS is not the only prep school option you may be offered. The Naval Academy Foundation sponsors 65-70 candidates each year to attend one of 22 private prep schools around the country. The Foundation provides scholarships based on need. As with NAPS, the Academy Admissions board identifies prep school candidates from those who applied to the Naval Academy but did not receive an appointment. Over 95 percent of Foundation prep-schoolers get an appointment after completing prep school.

Whether NAPS or another prep school, the year will be very well spent. Said one BGO, "If a candidate says, 'I'm not interested in prep school,' their motivation score goes down. How badly do they really want to go to the Naval Academy? Besides, it's a great deal. You get another year of maturity, another year of chemistry, and a better chance for a nomination and appointment to the Academy."

HOW TO SURVIVE

FOURTEEN
What To Expect During
The Rugged Plebe Year

The plebe year at the Naval Academy seems longer and more difficult than the plebes could have ever imagined. The upperclass seem to be intent on, and very skilled at, making plebes' lives miserable.

Why do they make it so hard? Do they want to weed out the weakest members of the herd, drive out those who are less than 100% committed, expose and reject those with character flaws?

The plebes may believe that to be true, but it is far from the truth. The Academy has invested as much time and energy into getting you appointed as you have. If you receive an appointment and show up on Indoctrination Day, everyone at the Academy wants you to succeed. Even the upperclassmen.

The odds are heavily in your favor. About 80 percent of those who enter go on to complete all four years and graduate.

But why the constant harassment? Why do plebes have to "chop" in the hallways (run with their knees up high)? Why do they have to flawlessly recite seemingly meaningless trivia from *Reef Points*? What does all that pressure accomplish?

FINDING YOUR LIMITS

As soon as you arrive for Plebe summer, you will be expected to memorize pages and pages of material—rates—from your *Reef Points* book. You will be asked about what happened in the news, the dinner menu, and countless other facts and trivia. No matter how smart you are, you can guarantee that you are not going to be able to do it all.

You will clean your room until you are certain that not a speck of dust remains. Then an upperclassman will get down on his knees and find dust under your bunk, or find a loose thread on your blouse, or a smudge on your shoes. You will constantly be reminded that you have not done all that is expected. Harsh criticism will be an accepted part of every day as a plebe.

Why are they asking you do to the impossible? The main reason is to prove to you that you can work much harder and accomplish much more than you ever thought possible. By setting the bar impossibly high, they will extend your reach.

They also want you to know your own limitations. An overconfident officer, like General Custer at Little Bighorn, is a danger to his people.

The officers and upperclassmen are making sure that when you are monitoring a submarine's nuclear reactor, or standing watch on a ship in a combat zone, or leading a platoon of Marines into battle, you will be at your

You will have to memorize pages and pages of information. USNA Photo Lab

best. You will be able to handle the most difficult missions. This is a lesson they want you to learn long before actual lives are at stake.

LESSONS IN TIME MANAGEMENT

Another thing that frustrates plebes is for upperclassmen to give them multiple tasks and about half enough time to get them done. It might seem pointless. But there is a solid rationale behind it.

The practice is intended to teach time management. As one midshipman explained, "Time management is absolutely key, realizing from the get-go that you aren't going to get everything done. Keep in mind what is the most important and focus in on that."

Once midshipmen graduate and become naval officers, they can be sure that their jobs will require good time management skills. They will have to juggle multiple tasks, prioritize those tasks, and make the best possible use of the hours in the day.

Almost every graduate interviewed for this book cited time management as one of the best life lessons they learned at the Academy.

FAILURE LEADS TO CONFIDENCE

Most midshipmen arrive at the Academy more accustomed to success than to failure. They always earned good grades, excelled in sports, and were recognized as leaders among their peers.

During their plebe year, however, they will almost surely come face to face with failure. The upperclassmen will be quick to remind plebes that they are falling short. They don't know their rates, they fail an inspection, or they neglect to accomplish a task that an upperclassman assigned.

For the first time they experience mental defeat. For those who have always been perfectionists, it can be a gut-wrenching experience. They are sure that they are not good enough. They question whether they belong at the Naval Academy, and whether they have what it takes to be a naval officer.

The Academy teaches plebes what it feels like to experience failure so that they will develop some of the

Plebes learn to pay close attention to the smallest details. USNA Photo Lab

attributes that are vital to a leader: resilience, tenacity, and humility.

If you go to the Naval Academy, you are almost guaranteed to perform poorly at something. Once you have experienced failure, you will no longer be afraid of failure. You will understand how to learn from your mistakes and move on. You will have the confidence to take on bigger challenges without holding back out of fear of failure. That kind of confidence is essential for military officers.

TEAMWORK

Many plebes come to the Naval Academy as strong individualists. Throughout high school, they have learned to do things on their own. They study alone and they work out alone. They distance themselves from their friends and classmates who may not be as hard-working or determined to succeed. They know that the most dependable person in their life is themselves.

The Naval Academy is designed to change people with this type of attitude. Why? Imagine life on an aircraft carrier. Everyone on board, from the mechanics to the cooks to the fighter pilots, depends on everyone else to work together. Those who cannot think and work as members of a team are not just ineffective—they are a threat to the safety of everyone else.

Said one mid, "I think the reason why a lot of people quit is because they don't know how to work well with others. One of the biggest things is being able to put your talents out there and work hard for other people, and a lot of people have a hard time justifying that."

Herndon is the ultimate test of teamwork.   USNA PHOTO LAB

It is no coincidence that the capstone exercise to the plebe year is the ultimate exercise in teamwork. Known as Herndon, the exercise takes place in May and requires the plebe class to work together to climb the 21-foot tall obelisk—which is covered in lard—and retrieve a "dixie cup" hat from the top. Tradition says whoever grabs the hat will be the first in the class to make admiral.

As they try to form a human pyramid, the plebes will be covered in lard and sweat. Herndon can take minutes or hours. It all depends on how well the plebes have learned to put aside their individualism and work together as a team.

When they can do that, they will have proven to the upperclassmen that they are ready to move past the plebe year.

The plebe year is not meant to weed out the weak; it is intended to take young men and women with outstanding potential and help them reach that potential. The plebe system is designed to strengthen plebes mentally, physically, and morally so they will develop the attitudes and traits of successful naval officers.

Before the plebe year is over, about 100 plebes will have left. About half will have left voluntarily. They are mostly those who were at the Academy for the wrong reasons, or those who did not understand what they were getting into.

Others are dismissed for a variety of reasons, such as misconduct, including honor violations, or poor military performance. Many leave because they have performed so poorly in academics that they are dismissed or they quit out of discouragement.

But the midshipmen themselves will tell you that if you work hard, do what is asked of you, and remained focused on your goals, you can survive. The following chapters give more specific advice on how to survive, and maybe even enjoy, your four years at the Naval Academy.

FIFTEEN
Advice From Plebes

Hundreds of plebes were interviewed during several visits to the Naval Academy. Most were interviewed in late winter and spring—after they had survived eight to ten months of plebe indoctrination. Some were interviewed just days before "Herndon," when one of them, with the help of classmates, would climb the Herndon Monument—the ritual that celebrates the end of the plebe year.

The same general comments were made to all of them: You survived, yet some 100 of your classmates did not. Why? And what have you learned from your experiences this year that can be passed on as advice to future plebes? A number of common ideas came up again and again.

ATTITUDE IS EVERYTHING

One of the most repeated comments had to do with attitude. Virtually every plebe stressed that survival was largely a matter of having the right attitude. What exactly does that mean?

Some stressed the importance of remembering the reason they are there in the first place. That may sound easy now, but many plebes commented on how hard it was in the midst of daily struggles and challenges. Said one plebe, "When it started getting rough during the academic year, I didn't understand why I was here any more. I lost my perspective. I think it's hard to gain it back, even now. You're always pushed in some way.

Live through one day at a time, but remember your goal: to become a naval officer.
USNA PHOTO LAB

"When I wake up at five-thirty in the morning I think, 'Why am I here.' That will go through your head tons of times. You have to have one single, solitary reason why you decided to come here. It can't be some lofty dream that I'm going to become an admiral someday. It has to be a more immediate goal. I want to be an officer. I want to be a pilot. You have to have a reason like that. You have to have the faith that that's why you're here."

Whether you came for one of the reasons listed in Chapter 4, or another reason, keeping that reason in mind will help you through the difficult times. Said another plebe, "I think everyone is here for a different reason. If you have a strong personal reason of why you want to be here, then you can get past the little annoyances."

An important perspective that came up repeatedly was to be mentally prepared for failure and criticism. This can be a real challenge for plebes who were used to being successful at everything in high school. Said one, "The biggest mistake I saw was the attitude of so many who thought they were the best. You come here and you'll find out you're not the best. You might have been a big shot in the town you came from, but here you are in with a thousand other people who were big shots just like you. The kinds who tried to be big shots here got cut right down to size and they weren't prepared to handle that at the beginning."

> *Dealing with failure is an important part of the Academy education; be mentally prepared for it.*

Another plebe echoed this idea, stressing that you have to be ready to fail at something: "Don't be afraid to fail. Be ready to accept failure and you'll have your head right when you do fail. Accept failure with the idea that now I'm going to do better. And remember, no matter what an upperclassman says to you, he can't kill you." Dealing with failure is an important part of the Academy education; be mentally prepared for it.

And be ready to get yelled at over what seems like the smallest detail: "I couldn't believe that the upperclassmen will get dirty looking for dirt—they will get down on their knees and get under the bed to find a speck of dust.

"Get ready for lots of nitpicking. I never expected their pickiness about the uniform—they can always find something. They tell you to get the strings off your white works [uniform] and I got some of them off. But at the first formation they looked in my pockets and pulled some strings out. They can find anything wrong so don't be surprised at how picky they are."

Many of the plebes emphasized the importance of keeping positive things in minds when the upperclassmen are getting you down.

Said one, "I kept at it a day at a time and tried not to look ahead—that's deadly—do not look ahead or the days will frighten you. The thing that really got me through this year was thinking of the positive things about this

Get ready for lots of nitpicking.   USNA Photo Lab

place. I kept going back in my mind to the goals I had when I came here—
I wanted an education and a job that I could be proud of—and a college that
I could be proud of. Like now, when I go home, there are adults coming up
to me and asking how it's going. They don't go up to my friends and ask
them how it's going at the University of Pennsylvania. I get satisfaction out
of that. I feel secure here. I know I'll have a job after I graduate—other
college graduates don't have that guarantee. I have my books and I can
concentrate on the things that are important here—I don't have to worry
about all the other things most college students worry about. Thinking about
all these positive things is what got me through plebe year."

DON'T TAKE IT PERSONALLY

You will make mistakes, and you will be criticized loudly and harshly
for those mistakes. As one plebe explained, "No matter what, you are not
going to come here and get out of getting flamed on. There's no way to
avoid it. They have to find something wrong with you. Even if there's
nothing wrong with you, they will find something wrong and you have to
accept that fact. You just have to put your head down and plow through it—
and then, well, I'm soon going to be shaking hands with those guys [who
were criticizing me]."

Another plebe explained, "I came in right out of high school and my
counselor had told me they were going to yell at me. But I didn't know they
would yell right in my face. I had a hard, hard time at the beginning because
of that. After about the first semester, you learn what's going to be expected;
then you know that they're going to yell at you about."

In the face of all this criticism, it is easy to begin feeling defensive. But many plebes emphasized not taking that criticism personally. "I think the hardest part for me was initially I started taking the things that the upper classmen would say personally. I know they say don't take those things personally, but over the summer I really let it get me down."

Expect plenty of mental pressure.
USNA PHOTO LAB

Another plebe repeated that idea, "The best advice for me was not to take it personally—the upperclassmen don't hate you; they're just doing their job. They want to make you a better midshipman."

All these opportunities for failure accompanied by constant criticism may seem designed to cause a total loss of confidence. But the opposite is true. The sooner you learn to be confident, or at least appear to be confident, the better off you will be.

In every group of plebes there is one or two who seems to draw more attention. They are called, "s—- screens," thought the offensive first word is usually dropped and the term shortened to "screen." One such plebe offered this personal story:

"I was a screen. During Plebe Summer I ranked 12th out of 12 in my squad. They then put me in a bad squad and I had to start to dig my way out—and I did, eventually. Later, I was first in my squad.

"My problem was that I was quiet to begin with, and it took me a while to learn how to yell. I could be just as tough as they were but I didn't have the command voice and they really got on me. You have to be confident in anything you do. When you say, 'I'll find out, sir!' [because you don't know an answer to a question] yell it in their face. If you know you're going to get in trouble, get your confidence up and be bold. Don't shake and shiver when being disciplined. Try not to show emotion—if you do start showing emotions they're going to make it harder."

Many plebes advised learning how to show confidence: "You don't have to answer right away when they ask you a question. Think about it; then draw yourself up and when you say it, say it with force and confidence. Someday you may have to tell some men to go risk their lives to take a hill and your voice has to maintain confidence. That's what they're training you for."

"The loud response also is tradition," said another plebe in response to the above comment. "Back in the days of the sailing ships and, later, in the noisy engine rooms, the ability to shout so you could be understood was an important part of being in the Navy. It's hard at first—it seems silly. But the quicker you get used to it, the easier it will be."

Another important way to avoid becoming a screen is to find ways NOT to draw extra attention to yourself. Blending in is a survival skill you must learn. One plebe explained it this way: "I think the most important thing that I learned over plebe summer—actually I was given this advice by someone who was in the Army—was that you just want to blend. Do not stick out. Don't be the first; don't be the last; just get by. If you're a high performer, everybody is going to be watching you. Then you screw up, and the hammer is going to fall. If you're always behind, the hammer is going to fall. If you're just that guy who is always going, you're going to be fine.

"Basically the analogy that I heard was as a plebe you're a zebra and all of the upperclassmen are lions. The big thing you had to do was stick with the herd. Occasionally, one or two of them are going to get pulled away from the herd, but if you can stay with the heard, especially through Plebe Summer, you'll be OK."

Being inconspicuous in the middle of the pack is a big change for plebes who were used to being out front in high school. As a plebe, the upperclassmen will be quick to let you know if you haven't learned this lesson well.

PLEBES TALK ABOUT TIME MANAGEMENT

Time management. Nearly every graduate cites this skill as one of the best lessons they learned at the Naval Academy. Nearly every midshipman cites time management as the biggest day-to-day challenge they face. They advise you to learn this lesson as soon as you can.

Explained one plebe, "I believe the hardest thing at the Academy is that there isn't an individual task that you have to do that just makes your life so miserable—it's all the individual tasks together. Everybody has said this in one way or another, but it is a stretch on your time. People push priorities on you and it's hard to figure out which one you want to do and which ones aren't as important to you. Definitely, each task put together into one day, that makes the hardest thing about this place."

Another explained that even if you try to plan your day carefully, something undoubtedly interferes with your plan: "I think probably one of the biggest problems here is there are so many things that you hear about five minutes before you're supposed to be there."

Yet another offered a similar thought: "One of the hardest things for me during the academic year, you would have your week planned out, 'I'm going to work on this English paper now, going to do this homework during the week,' but something comes up. I have to stand watch for two hours here and I have some mandatory brief to go to this night. Everything just gets pushed back."

Survival depends on being able to identify what task is most important, and staying flexible when your well-laid plan is disrupted.

KNOW WHAT TO EXPECT

This book is in your hands, so you have done at least one thing to try to learn more about what you will face as a plebe. The more you learn, the less you will be surprised, and the more you can focus on getting past the challenges in front of you. Talk to as many mids and graduates as you can, or cadets from West Point or the Air Force Academy, because their experiences are similar. Visit the Academy if you can.

One plebe admitted to being caught by surprise: "I honestly didn't know that the whole academic year was hard. I thought it was Plebe Summer and then I thought it would be like college. Nobody told me."

Many plebes advised learning as much as possible about what you are getting into: "Know what you're getting into before you get here, and accept it before you start—that's a huge thing. Expect the mental pressure to be tougher than you think and don't worry about the physical stuff—just be in decent shape. I didn't expect the memorizing and all that business. I didn't think it was going to be as bad as it was.

"Also, be ready for the heat and humidity during Plebe Summer. There were several days when it was over a hundred. It was so hot in the open that shooting with a rifle against your face was painful."

Some plebes also admitted that the Academy could not live up to their high expectations in every way. Some said they actually thought it would be tougher militarily. One expected every single midshipman to be a perfect role model: "Keep in mind that this place isn't perfect. I came here with stars in my eyes, thinking how nice it would be living in honor with people who want to serve their country. But you look around after awhile and you see upperclassmen that you can't respect. They're pushing the system and getting by with as little as possible. This was a shock for me and I was cynical for awhile. But I finally realized that I was just naïve. This place isn't perfect and it never will be. Be realistic in your expectations. As soon as I accepted the fact that this place isn't perfect, then I began to appreciate all the great people here even more."

KEEP YOUR SENSE OF HUMOR

Nearly every interview with a group of midshipman was a live demonstration of a key survival skill: a good sense of humor. If you can laugh at yourself, laugh at the things that seem trivial or absurd, the burden will seem a little lighter. As one plebe put it, "Keep your sense of humor about everything—laugh in your room with your roommates when you screw up."

Mental breaks can often come in the form of extra activities, getting involved in something you enjoy such as a club or sport, or even visiting

Try to keep your sense of humor.　　　　　　　　　　　USNA Photo Lab

your sponsor family. Said one plebe, "I would say a big thing that people should do when they get here to help is to get themselves away from the Academy as much as they can. Join some sport or some group to get you out of here so that you can get your mind off this place."

They also advise you to rely on the close friends that you will have. "All the positive things about this place help keep you here, but the greatest thing of all is the network of friends that you develop here. They are the key to survival. And you know that you will have these same friends for your whole career—wherever we go in the world we will meet old friends—the same network of friends we have right here."

A final word of advice came from another plebe, who said with a grin, "About all I'd tell my little brother [if he came here] is to be sure and memorize his social security number, and not to forget how to laugh!"

SIXTEEN
Upperclassmen Tell How To Survive

When upperclassmen give survival advice, that advice carries some added weight. Those upperclassmen have the advantage of taking a step back from their own plebe experiences, and perhaps looking at them with a broader perspective and added maturity. Upperclassmen have also watched the plebes who came after them, and have seen their struggles and successes.

Even with this advantage of perspective, much of their advice is strikingly similar to that of the plebes. In those cases, the advice is valuable enough that you will benefit from hearing it again, in slightly different words.

MAJOR ADJUSTMENTS

Life at the Naval Academy is so different from the life most plebes led before I-Day that when they talk to their friends back home, they have a hard time putting it all into words. Within a matter of days, the old life of watching TV on the couch, running to McDonald's for a burger, and text-messaging and IM-ing friends all afternoon are a long-distant memory.

According to some of the upperclassmen, coping with this drastic change is tough for some plebes.

Homesickness can be a problem for any college freshman, and the Naval Academy is no exception. Explained one first classman, "For the past year, I have been one of the guys in the company who has had to help the plebes solve some of [their] problems. The biggest problem was homesickness, especially this summer. I had one plebe after just three days who was so down that he didn't know what to do and he wanted to talk to mom and dad [which is forbidden except at certain times]. He was at the low point of his whole life.

"I called him into my room, sat him down, and one-on-one I told him what the purpose of the Academy was and what we were trying to do during Plebe Summer. But he was bawling his eyes out because he was scared. I was as sympathetic as I could be because I could remember being in the same exact position, but I maintained our professional relationship and let him get it all out. Then, instead of saying it's going to be alright, I turned it around and I made him start thinking about why he was here and what he was going to do."

For many plebes, the most difficult adjustment is adapting to the complete loss of freedom—having every minute and every aspect of their lives dictated by someone else. Meanwhile, their friends from high school who are attending civilian colleges are enjoying more freedom than ever. When they compare notes through phone calls or e-mails, the plebes often feel they are missing out on too much.

Be prepare for a complete loss of freedom. USNA PHOTO LAB

Explained one upperclassman, "When I finally got home for Thanksgiving [my plebe year], I was so happy, then rolled into Army week after that, then Christmas break and that is just a solid good month. But then you have to come back for three months where you're not allowed to go out again. That was the hardest part for me. Just how long it was away from family and friends, being able to go places and do what you want, freedom to drive around on your own. That was definitely the hardest part of the year for me."

Said an international student from Ireland, "Your day is planned. You get up, everything is planned. You don't have enough time to go back to your room and just chill, relax, and talk. Lights out. Then it starts again."

What is the upperclassmen's advice on dealing with these difficult adjustments? Two recommendations were repeated again and again.

First, remember why you are there. "That's a key survival tool for this place—having goals. Part of the preparation coming into plebe year is to say to yourself, 'Why am I going to the Academy.' And to survive, your reason should be, 'I am going to become a professional officer in the naval service.'" Said another, "As long as you really wanted to do it [make it through the plebe year], you were able to stick with it and bear through the tough spots."

The second recommendation may seem like a direct contradiction to the first goal of keeping your long-term goal in mind. When facing each day, upperclassmen recommend you concentrate on one day at a time, or one challenge at a time. Said one, "You have to keep the big picture and live just for today." Said another, "Be able to pull yourself together. Once you can do it one time, you are ready for the rest of the time." Commit yourself to doing the best you can to make it through that one day, and eventually the days will add up and the plebe year will end.

DID I MENTION TIME MANAGEMENT?

Getting through each day means more than just surviving, however. As you concentrate on each day, if you are going to succeed, you will have to make the most out of every minute.

You may be thinking, "I feel like I already read this section." Perhaps that is because many of the graduates interviewed in Chapter 3 talked about the importance of time management skills, as did the professors in Chapter 6 and the plebes in Chapter 15. And you will hear more on this subject in later chapters ... because at the Naval Academy, time management is THAT IMPORTANT!

In the words of one upperclassman, "[The hard part] was how much you had to do and also how little time you had. You just have to manage your own workout schedule; you have to work on the professional things you have to do, interviews, briefs, anything else that comes your way, because things will come at the last minute. Everything constantly gets shifted, all the time. You have to be careful about that and make sure you stay on top of things. Once you fall behind a little bit, it takes an eternity to catch up."

The quicker you learn this lesson, the easier your plebe year will be.

IT'S HARD TO BE HUMBLE

One of the reasons plebes get frustrated as they learn Naval Academy-style time management is that they have to let go of being perfect at everything they do. They succeeded in high school—and earned an appointment to the Naval Academy—by striving to be the best at everything. Now they find themselves having to choose between memorizing rates and going over their chemistry assignment one more time.

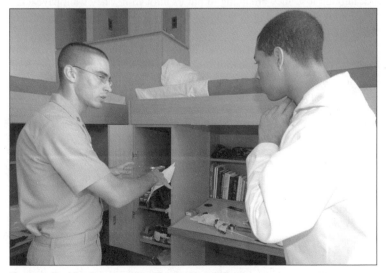

No matter how hard you try, you will experience failure.   USNA PHOTO LAB

Explained one upperclassman, "You have to decide that this assignment has top priority and this other assignment just may not get done. Of course, in doing this, you have to be ready to take your lumps in some classes. Those who have been conscientious students really fight this."

Taking your lumps is part of the curriculum. Be ready to be humbled. "If you come here, try not to let your ego get the best of you. A lot of kids walk around sticking their chests out saying look at me, look at me, I'm awesome. The reality is, you are not."

Upperclassmen advise you to be ready to experience failure, be ready to be humbled and learn from your mistakes. "I know lots of people who got the first F they ever got in their life at this place. But you have to grow from that. You have to look at yourself and say, 'I did my best and failed; now what did I learn from that?' Then go on."

THE LEADERSHIP LABORATORY

Plebes are not the only midshipmen who make mistakes. And academic tests are not the only tests at the Naval Academy.

Every midshipman is learning something about leadership every day. Plebes are learning how to follow and be part of a team. Upperclassmen are learning how to set goals and motivate others. The upperclassmen recommend that when you are being yelled at and it does not make sense to you, keep in mind that everyone is part of this leadership laboratory.

As one explained, "I think that sometimes the upperclassmen are trying to learn to be leaders, but I find a lot of the people that I was led by thought it was just a game. 'Oh, we're going to have fun with you guys.' They were put through it so they are going to put us through it. They want payback. I don't think they're going to lead people like that when they [graduate and] go to the fleet."

Remember that the person yelling at you is learning too, and you will be less frustrated. You can learn from their mistakes, not just your own. Said another upperclassman, "I think during the academic year you can see people actually trying to do some leadership and learn leadership styles. When you get more used to it, you start noticing leadership styles, where before you just do whatever anybody says."

WORTH THE PRICE

Looking back at their plebe year, nearly all upperclassmen will tell you that what they gained was well worth the struggles they endured.

One first classman had this to say:

"Coming to the Naval Academy was the best decision I ever made in my life. The system is designed to build people who are strong and can handle pressure—people who have the guts to hang in there when the going gets tough. That's what this place is about—and the positive attitude is

Those midshipman who stick it out until graduation are always glad they did.

USNA PHOTO LAB

what's going to help you make it. I was once at the ultimate low, ready to be kicked out. Now I have the class ring; I'm starting my senior year; I'm well respected by my peers and subordinates; and this is because I hung in there and trusted the system.

"And what would I tell a candidate if he asked me what is the best thing about this place?

"I would tell him that it's a place where you'll find out who you are."

SEVENTEEN
Academic Survival Tips

Upperclass pressure is only part of the stress of plebe life. Many plebes struggle to keep up with the academic demands at the Academy. In fact, the midshipmen who did the best in high school often have the most problems. They never learned how to study efficiently—they were able to get good grades just by listening in class and doing the required homework.

Those who had to work hard in high school to get good grades, and those who attended college or a prep school before coming to the Naval Academy, experience less academic shock. Perhaps they came from a demanding school with high standards; perhaps they developed good work habits for some other reason. Said one, "I lived out in the country with nothing else to do and I just got into the habit of outlining every book as we went through them. I had no idea how much that habit would help me when I got here."

We already talked about academic shock, and ways to prepare academically, in Chapter 5 and Chapter 6. The goal of this chapter is to give you academic survival advice you can use once you get to the Academy. The advice comes from a variety of midshipmen, some who had to work very hard to pull themselves out of academic trouble.

You may find that some of the advice is conflicting, and you may also find that not all of it makes sense for you. But as you read all these comments, think how you might adapt the techniques and recommendations for yourself.

FOCUS

The first comments are from a first classman who was also a football player. "The most important thing of all is so important it should be a rule that is adopted by every plebe. Always put your mind where you are at. That means when you are on the football field, think only about football and nothing else. Then, when you are in chemistry class, think only about chemistry and nothing else.

"That might seem simplistic to a plebe, but it's really not that simple, especially when you have so little time and so many demands upon it. But if you follow the rule, you will focus 100 percent on whatever you're doing, and you'll try to achieve as much as possible with that time. In chemistry class, focus 100 percent on what's going on and learn as much as you can in the class. Don't just say, 'Hey, I'll listen to this guy and pick up what I don't understand when I get back to my room.' That's a trap. Don't let anything go by you in class that you don't understand. Ask questions and stay alert.

Give it your best concentration. Then, when you go to English class, do the same thing.

"Take notes intensively in class. It's real easy just to sit and listen. You say, 'Oh yeah, I understand everything he's saying.' You do, but two days later you've forgotten; then you have to dig it out of the book. Also, while you're taking notes, listen carefully and the prof' will tell you the questions that are going to be on the next test.

"Another advantage of taking thorough notes is that it keeps you awake. You can't imagine how tired you get around here and it's easy to fall asleep. But when you take good notes, it keeps you alert and that is important."

Keeping your focus includes knowing when you should close the books and go to bed, so that you can be awake and alert the next day. It also includes knowing how to take short mental breaks, then get back to work.

PRIORITIZE

As you lay out your study schedule each day, you will often find that you will not be able to get everything done. Instead, you must learn to prioritize your efforts. The football player continued with this advice, "Those who have been conscientious students really fight this, but I would tell any candidate to get it in your head that you're rarely going to have enough time to do everything that you want to do, especially that first year when the upperclassmen are pressuring you to learn your rates. If the plebes could just get over this mental hurdle quickly, they would be so much better off."

Nearly every midshipmen interviewed talked about the need to prioritize. That may mean working on the class you enjoy least and neglecting your favorite subject. It may mean going to a class unprepared for a pop quiz. Prioritizing is an art form you will have to practice.

Said a plebe, "You have to be ready to take the hit. Say I've got an English assignment due tomorrow and also a quiz in chemistry. I have to decide maybe to study the chemistry and to blow off the English assignment and take the hit in English the next day. Those are the kinds of decision that you're always having to make."

One of the main problems for plebes is the conflict between learning the professional material assigned by upperclassmen—the "pro stuff" and rates—and the academic homework. Said a second classman, "The problem is that the upperclassmen give you these assignments like, 'Give a ten minute oral report on a hand grenade.' Well, you're living with them [the upperclassmen, not the grenade!], and the prof's are over in the other buildings, so there is always that extra pressure to do the pro stuff or know the rate rather than study for academics. Many plebes get themselves in trouble because they forget to balance it out."

A plebe who went to prep school said he learned a technique for achieving that balance: "What I really learned at NAPS is to follow a

Many midshipmen find it helpful to study with classmates; others prefer a quiet place free of all distractions.   USNA PHOTO LAB

routine. They had me programmed. I studied the pro stuff from seven until eight. Then I knocked it off and hit the books at eight."

ELIMINATE DISTRACTIONS

Since your study time is so scarce and so valuable, it makes sense to maximize every minute. Midshipmen had plenty of advice on how to avoid the many distractions plebes can encounter.

The number one, most often-repeated piece of advice: "Go to the library." As one midshipman explained, "The more time I was spending in my room, the less work I was getting done. Either because of stuff on the computer or my roommate, or upperclass will come by and say you have to do something…there are just a lot of distractions.

"First semester, our [the plebes in my company] grades weren't that good, so we weren't allowed to be in Bancroft Hall during study hour. It actually helped so much. I mean, personally, my grades improved a lot. As soon as study hour started, everybody would leave, go to the library or whatever. It does help a lot."

Others suggested an empty room in an academic building rather than the library. Said one, "I'm a people person. I like going to the library because there are a whole bunch of people there. But for some people being around people, they get distracted, talk here, talk there. I know sometimes I go to Luce [one of the academic buildings], the top floor, close all the blinds and all, close the door, put a chair in front of the door, and do my work there. It was like I'm not getting out until I finish."

The exact location is less important than the principle: "Get rid of all distractions when you sit down to study."

LOST IN CYBERSPACE:
E-MAIL, INSTANT MESSAGING, FACEBOOK, & COMPUTER GAMES

One of the biggest distractions that tempt the plebes is the computer. It can provide you a needed mental break from the demands of Academy life. Your computer can connect you instantly to your friends from high school, your family, your boyfriend or girlfriend. It can transport you to a fantasy world where no one is yelling at you.

Explained one upperclassman, "The reason people do it, at least with Facebook I know, is the feeling of separation. You want to see what your friends are doing. If you are stuck here doing the same thing over and over again, you want to get sort of a reminder of what life was like back then, outside of here."

Cell phones can be another big temptation. Said another, "I'm not saying it's bad to have relationships or anything, but one of the hardest things here is when you're sitting at your desk doing homework, it's really hard to open that math book when you can sit on your cell phone and talk to your friends."

All midshipmen's computers should come with a warning label: CAUTION, BLACK HOLE! That black hole can suck you in and cause hours of study time to be lost forever.

How to stay out of this black hole? The mids have plenty of advice.

1. **Set a schedule.** One mid suggested, "Just allot yourself some personal time during the night. If you're going to goof off, say 'I'm going to goof off now, but only for like 15 minutes,' and then get back to work." Said another, "I went through an AIM stage in high school when I was 16. I realized it's such a waste of time. I had that going for me when I came in here, knowing all that internet stuff is just bad news. I still have AIM but I only use it on weekends and stuff."

Some midshipmen set a time, such as Sunday afternoons, to call Mom and Dad or their friends back home. Then they leave the cell phone off for the rest of the week.

2. **Watch out for each other.** One mid explained, "Having a roommate just get on your case about it, just kind of watch over you a little bit, it helps."

3. **Organize and prioritize.** One mid had a well-organized system for sorting out e-mail traffic: "With my e-mail account, I definitely have two. I have one hotmail account and one that's my mids account. I have everything sorted so the junkmail typically goes to the hotmail account and everything else goes to my mids account. In that account, I have different folders for academics, company stuff, and other things, and I sort it like that."

Another expanded on this idea, "You have to be an e-mail profiler. You have to go down through the lists, see people whose e-mails are clearly not going to be important, and just erase them right away."

4. **Eliminate temptation.** Some mids know that the black hole is a powerful force, so they come up with ways to avoid temptation completely. Said one, "The best way to alleviate the threat of cyberspace would just be getting out of Bancroft Hall."

Another mid suggested deleting tempting programs: "I have a lot of games like solitaire, free cell, that type of stuff. I eventually deleted it off my computer just because it was such a distraction with all the other stuff—MySpace, all that other fun jazz."

Yet another put it in very blunt language: "My advice for people coming in: don't sign up for Facebook. Don't even do it. Get away from a computer. They are just a big threat. My grades have dropped significantly since I joined Facebook. That sounds pathetic, but it's true."

As with all the tips in this chapter, you will have to figure out which of these work best for you. Be aware of how you study best and how addicting cyberspace is for you, and work out a plan that protects you from becoming lost in the black hole of cyberspace.

ASK FOR HELP

When the challenges of the Academy seem overwhelming, keep a few things in mind. First, the demanding admissions process ensures that those who receive appointments have the ability to succeed. Second, only a small percentage of midshipmen—about 4 percent—leave for academic reasons.

Third, help is there for the asking. The officers and professors at the Academy want you to succeed. More than that, your success is their mission, their reason for being assigned to the Naval Academy. Your classmates and even the upperclassmen want you to succeed, and they will help you as much as they can.

One of the most unique attributes of Academy professors is their availability. The will meet one on one with midshipman for extra instruction, or EI, during free periods. Some will even give EI on weekends or in the evenings, and some will take phone calls at home as well. Many midshipman claim they would not have survived chemistry or calculus without abundant EI sessions.

Another advantage of EI is that is shows your professor that you are serious about the class. When your grade is on the border line, the professor's positive impression can often help.

Another resource is the Center for Academic Excellence, which provides everything from lessons in time management and note-taking, to tutoring in the more technical subjects. "It's good," said one midshipman, "once you start really dropping in a subject, like chemistry or calculus. My roommate used it a lot. They set him up with a tutor."

One of the most unique attributes of Academy professors is their availability to give you extra help if you need it.   USNA PHOTO LAB

Many midshipmen are more comfortable getting help from their peers. A formalized program known as Midshipmen Study Groups fills this gap. Study group leaders are midshipmen who have already taken and passed the course; they also receive special training in how to lead the groups.

Informal help from peers is also valuable. Said one, "The hardest class academically is chemistry, for me. It takes a group effort every time. You would get these web assignments on line, Web-assign. It seemed like our whole company was together the night it was due, working on the deadline."

Remember, once you get into the Naval Academy, surviving is primarily a function of your motivation. If you truly want to succeed, graduate, and become a naval officer, you will find ways to survive. There are tens of thousands of Academy graduates doing everything from commanding submarines to running businesses. Many of them suffered frustrations and setbacks. But they made it because they wanted to make it. You can, too.

EIGHTEEN
Getting Along With Classmates And Roommates

During interviews, midshipmen were asked to describe the worst and best things about the Naval Academy. Many agreed that the worst thing about the Naval Academy is the complete loss of personal freedom. Others had different answers.

And the best thing about the Naval Academy? Most agreed that the best thing is the extraordinary friendships that develop. Said one plebe, "Whenever I would be having tough times, when I would start getting down on the place, it would be my close friends that would bring me up."

These are friendships that last a lifetime, friendships strengthened by adversity, by enduring and helping one another through good and bad times.

On Induction Day, 1,300 strangers get sorted into squads and platoons and companies. One of their first assignments is to learn the names and hometowns of every person in their squad. These are the names of the people who will help them survive Plebe Summer. Plebes are taught from day one the importance of looking out for one another.

NEVER BILGE A CLASSMATE

Never bilge a classmate. This phrase might not make sense now. But within a few days of arriving at the Academy, you will accept it as a commandment that governs every minute of your day.

What does it mean? Said one thirdclassman, "The rule here is that you never bilge a classmate or a roommate. That means you should never try to make yourself look better than a classmate or a roommate.

"As an example, when the upperclassmen are grilling one of your classmates in the hall and she doesn't know a rate, you would never step up and say, 'I know it, sir.' That would be bilging. You would be trying to make yourself look good at the expense of a classmate.

"Another example is when three roommates are standing an inspection of their room. Your bed might be made perfectly, and so might the bed of another roommate. But if the upperclassmen find that the third bed is not up to the standards of the other two, it is the two plebes [with the good beds] who will catch hell. The beds that were made are ripped up and the two plebes are hacked.

"The reason? If you know how to make a bed that well, why haven't you helped your roommate learn the same thing?"

Why is this commandment so important? Future naval officers must learn a new mindset, a mindset of being responsible for one another and

Learning to work together is an important lesson for plebes.   USNA Photo Lab

everything that takes place in their unit. In combat or on a cruise, if one person doesn't do his or her job, the entire unit or ship can suffer. Midshipmen are taught to recognize when something needs to be done, and do it. All tasks are shared responsibilities.

As one mid explained, "Any name on the door [of your room], it's your fault. I remember I was actually late to my professional board because my room was not completely set in Bravo [inspection order] because my roommates had gone."

Said another third classman, "Another thing you never do is leave a roommate behind. Even when you have uniform races where everybody tries to change from whites into PE gear in two minutes, you never step outside that room without your roommate. Even if you're going to be late. If you show up without a roommate, that's a bilge.

"It's the same thing when you are doing something with a bunch of your classmates. If someone is dragging, you go help them. You carry something for them or you encourage them. You're bilging your classmates if you go off and leave them."

Helping each other extends beyond military duties to every aspect of the Academy. Many midshipmen and graduates credit their classmates with helping them survive academically. Said one mid, "There was a [midshipman in my company] who would sit in on a Calculus II class during one of his free periods so that he could help the rest of my classmates. A lot of people are there to help. They are more than willing to help out."

CLOSE QUARTERS: GETTING ALONG WITH ROOMMATES

You will probably share a room with one or two of your classmates. You may not have any say in who you room with. Nevertheless, you will depend on each other to help get your room and uniforms in inspection order. You may help each other with homework if one of you is stronger in a subject than the other. You will help cheer each other up when one of you is feeling down.

If one of you is not pulling your weight, or you have a disagreement or personality clash, the plebe year could be much harder. So all midshipmen will tell you to resolve to work through your differences and get along.

Said a second classman, "It is important to open up with your roommates and communicate. You run into trouble when one of them is unhappy or thinks something is wrong but won't communicate the problem. If you have a problem, you have to get it out. You should always let your roommates know how you are feeling and they should do the same. When you keep it inside, the pressure builds up, then hard feelings, and sooner or later, something will break down and you all will pay the price."

A first classman explained, "Roommates have to work together or it's very difficult to survive. If I don't feel like cleaning up the room, you're going to have to do it if you're my roommate. That's bad, because when upperclassmen come by, you can't bilge me; you just have to say, when asked why the room is dirty, 'no excuse, sir!' even though it's your lazy roommate's fault."

Said another, "It also helps to divide up the workload according to who does things best. Like before an inspection, one guy who can do a good rack [bed] does all three of them. Another who can wax the deck [floor] well does that. What you don't want is a guy who's a slob. But, if you get one, you just have to communicate and work it out."

Some roommates have more trouble than others getting along. Said one plebe, "I have this problem right now that I can't find a way to solve. As a female, you don't have that many choices for roommates [because of the small number of women in each company]. You can't change, and whoever you get to live with, that's who you're gong to live with for a very, very long time. So all I do is suck it up and go on. If you always have little squabbles, that won't help. You have to wait until things are calm before talking things out."

Another plebe had a similar experience: "My roommate right now doesn't clean up his stuff. I've told him nicely that if he doesn't put his stuff away when he leaves the room, I'm just going to throw it out. I put his stuff out in the hallway next to the garbage and he got [mad]. It worked. It was a little aggressive but sometimes you have got to make a point. He got his stuff together."

Said a second classman, "Everbody learns sooner or later to do the big things in the room—cleaning and making the beds, etc. But it's the little things that make the difference between good and bad roommates. A good roommate anticipates problems and takes steps to solve them. If my roommate sees that I'm late getting to the room when I have a formation, he anticipates all the things that I'm going to need. He lays out my uniform and checks it for lint, or he checks my shoes and if they need it, he shines them. It's these kinds of things that mean a lot. When roommates look out for each other like that, a close bond develops. That's how really close friendships develop. And that attitude, which is common throughout the Brigade, is what I love about this place."

The best thing about the Naval Academy is the friendships that develop.

USNA Photo Lab

Those friendships are what many midshipman and graduates love most about the place. When asked how they stuck with the Academy through the hard times, such as returning from Christmas break to the "dark ages" of winter, many midshipmen cited the friendships they had at the Academy. The bonds that had developed were much stronger than any of the hardships they faced, and last much longer than the four years they spent together at the Naval Academy.

NINETEEN
Advice For Intercollegiate Athletes

About 30 percent of midshipmen will be varsity athletes for all or part of their four years at Annapolis. Their lives are even more jam-packed than those of the other 70 percent of the brigade of midshipmen. And there is no comparison between the lives of midshipmen athletes and their civilian counterparts at State U.

Consider the intercollegiate athletes' life at a civilian school. They may take 12 semester hours, or four classes, arranged to accommodate their practice schedule. Some days, say on Tuesdays and Thursdays, they may have only one or maybe even no classes, so they can focus 100 percent on their sport. On weekends when they aren't traveling, they may sleep late or catch up on their studies.

In contrast, an athlete at the Academy will take the same course load as other midshipmen—about 18 hours on average—including classes like calculus, chemistry, and electrical engineering. They may miss the lunch formation to have team meetings or lift weights. They will scramble to the gym as soon as their classes are done for afternoon practice.[1]

After practice, physically exhausted, they head back to dinner, attend to military duties with their companies, and then finally sit down to wrestle with a big pile of homework. Exhausted, they drop into bed and get some sleep before starting all over again the next day. For the midshipman athlete, weekends may include practices or games, along with more military training, or meeting with an instructor or helpful classmate to catch up on work they missed while on a trip.

When Thanksgiving finally comes and most midshipmen get to go home and relax with mom and dad, many athletes find themselves on a bus to a tournament or game.

Most of these athletes had other options. They could play sports at a civilian school, perhaps even on scholarships. Many of them never thought about serving in the Navy or Marine Corps when they were in high school. What are they doing at the United States Naval Academy?

WHY ATHLETES CHOOSE THE NAVAL ACADEMY

Most midshipmen athletes come in two distinct varieties. The first are those who have wanted to attend the Naval Academy and serve their country for as long as they can remember. The fact that they are athletes may have

---

1. The Academy will try to schedule athletes' classes so they have the last period of the day free in order to get to practice. In reality, that isn't always possible.

helped them get into the Academy, but it is secondary to their desire to become naval officers. Their sport may provide a diversion from the less enjoyable aspects of Academy life, or an outlet for their competitive natures, but nothing more.

As one tennis player explained, "The reason to come here is to serve in the military. Sports help pass the time, but they aren't the reason for being here." A member of the track team echoed that idea: "Athletics is a tool to help get you here, and help get you when you're here. But it shouldn't be the only reason you come here. Athletics should be secondary. After four years, your athletic career is probably over."

The Naval Academy offers quality training facilities.
USNA Photo Lab

Not every midshipman starts out with that mindset. Some are motivated solely by the opportunity to play Division I college sports. Many never heard of the Naval Academy until their high school coach suggested it, or an Academy coach began to recruit them. They begin Plebe Summer and look in the mirror to see themselves with short hair and military uniforms, never having fully considered what it means to attend a service academy.

Attending a service academy means you will commit a good chunk of your young adult life to military service, but some athletes ignore that fact until they get to the Academy. A soccer player explained, "I had no military experience. But Navy was my best option. I was looking at smaller Division I or else Division II or III schools. I wouldn't have signed up for the whole nine years [four years at USNA and five as an officer] at the beginning, but I thought I would always wonder if I didn't give it a try. You have two years to decide whether you want to go into the Navy."

Some of the Naval Academy staff, as well as some of the midshipmen, will tell you that it doesn't matter why you come. An athlete can be lured mainly by the opportunity to play sports and still turn into a good officer. As one senior explained, "They are trying to recruit great athletes who can become good mids." In other words, the attributes that made you a good athlete—discipline, competitiveness, teamwork—combined with the experiences you gain at the Naval Academy often create very dedicated midshipmen and officers. As one put it, "I didn't really think about joining the military. After the first year, though, I was here for the right reasons."

One other common reason athletes choose the Naval Academy: Midshipmen athletes often share a realistic, long-range view that goes beyond college and sports. They understand the very small odds of playing professional sports or making a career out of their athletic interests and abilities. They realize that at any time, an injury could end their athletic careers. They know that a good education, the opportunity to reach their potential, and a guaranteed job after college are tremendous assets.

A final word of warning: If your sport is your one and only focus, the Naval Academy may not be for you. You will have too many competing demands that interfere with your sport. And every day, you will be reminded that you are first and foremost a midshipman—not just a linebacker, a pitcher, or a forward.

Life in the post-9/11 Navy has made that even more true. All midshipmen are conscious of the fact that they will serve in a wartime Navy or Marine Corps. While some graduates have managed to pursue professional sports, as of this writing the Navy will not consider athletes' requests to leave the service before they have served for at least two years. As one football player explained, "The Naval Academy's mission is to provide combat effective leaders. Keep that in mind. You're not here to be in the NFL. If you don't want to serve, go somewhere else."

Many athletes, however, find the Naval Academy a perfect fit.

HOW ATHLETES DO IT ALL IN A 24-HOUR DAY

For many midshipmen, Plebe Summer is the hardest thing they have ever been through. Most midshipmen athletes, in contrast, will tell you Plebe Summer was the easy part. First, most athletes are well prepared for the physical challenges of Plebe Summer. They normally do not struggle with the running and calisthenics. Also, many athletes adjust easily to the mental stress, having faced tough and demanding coaches in high school.

One senior explained, "Getting through Plebe Summer being an athlete, you've had abusive coaches, you were hazed as a high school freshman. But if you play team sports, you're two steps ahead as a plebe, from what you learned in high school." His classmate agreed: "Physically it wasn't too hard. You already have an attitude of working with others, and you're used to being yelled at."

Many midshipmen must learn teamwork at the Naval Academy, and sometimes it is a very hard lesson to learn. For athletes, however, teamwork is already ingrained in their personalities. Working together is almost instinctive. Being competitive and being able to take criticism are also advantages during Plebe Summer.

Once the school year starts, life gets much harder. Most midshipmen athletes will tell you that academics are the biggest challenge they face. According to one senior, "Academics are the hardest thing about the Naval

Academy. I didn't realize how technical the course load is. If I had, I would have prepared better in high school." Said another, "The academic year is harder because of all the things you have to balance. I didn't get done with meetings or practice until 7:30. Sometimes I was up until two or four in the morning studying." Missing classes to travel with the team creates an added challenge.

Fortunately, most learn very quickly how to manage every minute of their time. Said one, "I quickly learned to go 100 miles per hour all the time. I use my free periods to study because at night I'm too tired to concentrate for three hours." In fact, many athletes report doing better academically during the on-season because "the less time you have to waste, the less time you waste. It's class—practice—dinner—homework." Midshipmen athletes get into high gear and stay there, and manage to get it all done.

The Naval Academy also provides plenty of extra help for those who want it, and that certainly applies to athletes. Explained one, "Football has a study hall in the evening for those who are struggling. And the professors understand [the demands of athletics]. They appreciate the work you put into it, so they make themselves available." Others seek help from roommates, classmates, or upperclassmen who are strong academically.

Sports also provide a needed break from the stresses of military training, especially during the plebe year. In the military environment of Bancroft Hall, plebes are criticized constantly, and are not allowed to form friendships with upperclassmen. That strict class distinction does not exist on the practice field, and many plebes enjoy that break. Said one athlete, "Lacrosse was my safe haven. I couldn't wait to get to practice and get treated like a normal person."

MIDSHIPMAN OR ATHLETE? HOW TO GET ALONG

The Naval Academy is an institution that encourages uniformity and conformity. Yet the four year experience of a midshipman athlete is obviously very different from those of his or her non-athlete classmates. Consider the following scenario:

From the moment he crawled out of bed at 0530, Midshipman Fourth Class Smith has been wondering what he is doing at the Naval Academy instead of State U. He had to scramble to get his room in inspection order, shower, and get dressed before going out in the hall to call chow.[2] After a long day of classes, most of them more challenging than he ever imagined, he will return to his company for more unfavorable attention from upperclassmen determined to train him into the best plebe possible.

---

2. Plebes must take turns standing at attention in the hallway to announce how much time remains before each meal or formation. This is also an opportunity to get quizzed on "rates" or be criticized for the condition of their uniform.

His roommate, Midshipman Fourth Class Jones, meanwhile, was not there to clean the room or suffer beside his classmates or have his day ruined by constant criticism. Mr. Jones was on a soccer trip, far from the Academy, joking around with the upperclassmen as if he were a real human being.

Mr. Jones is also wondering why he isn't at State U. He has been practicing extra hard, trying to earn a spot on the varsity roster. After running around the soccer field for three and a half hours every afternoon, he is almost too exhausted to do his homework at night. While his buddies were home over Thanksgiving eating mom's turkey dinner and catching up with friends, Jones was on a bus, on the way to a soccer game. He is missing the review session before the upcoming calculus test, a review he could really use. He will try to study on the way back to the Academy, but the bus will probably be too noisy and he will be much too tired. So he will be starting another week exhausted and behind.

He envies his roommate, who ought to be all caught up on his studies and well rested for the week ahead.

> "There's a little bit of tension. Usually it's just good natured jabs."

It is true that athletes and other midshipmen, especially plebes, have two different Academy experiences. That difference is unavoidable. But does that difference create tension or resentment between athletes and non-athletes? It depends. It depends on whom you ask, and how the athletes approach their military responsibilities.

Athletes do miss some of the parades and military training that other midshipmen have to attend, and the other midshipmen notice. Said one athlete, "There's a little bit of tension. Usually it's just good natured jabs. People joke about it." Non-athletes sometimes have misperceptions about the glamorous or privileged life of athletes. Another commented, "They say athletes are 'lucky' to get to travel. But you never have free time to go out to dinner. I've had maybe one free block of time on trips in two years."

But most athletes I interviewed feel their classmates understand the demands of playing intercollegiate sports. Said a member of the cross-country team, "They joke that we have an easier time, but they understand the work we put into it. Sometimes I'd rather do a parade than a workout. They appreciate it's a lot to juggle." A football player agreed, "They understand we only get a week off in the summer, we don't get Thanksgiving. There is a perception that we don't get along, but it's really not the case." Athletes also acknowledge that other midshipmen have responsibilities they do not. "The brigade commander has stacks of paperwork, lots to do as well."

Still, many athletes are conscious of the need to do all they can to participate in military training, to avoid any appearance of special treatment. "If you do what you need to do, make it known you want to help, [you'll get along]. If you act like you're special, try to get out of things, they'll see through you." Some take awhile to learn that lesson: "As a freshman I tried to get out of everything. The second year, I tried to be around and involved, so I got more respect. The plebes see you involved and follow your example. If you try to help, it goes a long way."

Since many athletes come to the Academy motivated by sports more than military service, other midshipman may question an athlete's reason for being there. Several athletes expressed that they felt they had to prove their motivation. Explained one athlete, "There was a stigma that I didn't come here for the right reasons. You [athletes] have to prove yourself to the cadre, maybe work harder. You have to create a clean slate." Most agreed that over the course of the four years, as they all matured and got to know each other better, mutual respect developed.

THE ATHLETES SPEAK

Vice Admiral John "Boomer" Stufflebeem, Class of 1975. Admiral Stufflebeem earned the nickname "Boomer" for his skills as a punter for Navy, and after graduation was signed with the Detroit Lions for four years. He went on active duty and realized his dream of becoming a Navy fighter pilot. He commanded Carrier Air Wing ONE in the Balkans and Arabian Gulf and Carrier Group TWO and Task Force Sixty during Operation IRAQI FREEDOM. He also served as military aide to President George H.W. Bush. Most recently, Admiral Stufflebeem was commander of the Sixth Fleet, and he is now Director of Navy Staff at the Pentagon.

VADM Stufflebeem at a meeting of NATO commanders. NATO

I had always been interested in serving in the military, and I really wanted to be a naval aviator. I had sailed in the Chesapeake Bay with my father, who was also in the Navy, while he was stationed in Washington, D.C. So I was impressed that the Naval Academy was the best way to reach my goals.

So I asked, "How do I get where I want to go?" I had heard that coming from the fleet was the easiest way, so I enlisted and went to boot camp. I was a drilling reservist for a year, I was activated a year later, and then attended the Naval Academy Prep School.

The Prep School was perfect for me. I wasn't the strongest academic student who had ever applied. NAPS helped me with my college board scores. I also found the academic courses during my first semester at the Naval Academy were about the same as at Prep School.

Because of my year at the Prep School I started very strong that first semester, and I finished strong my last semester, but my academic career was a bit of a sine wave in between. I like to say that I graduated #1 in the second half of my class! The academic program is difficult and I struggled.

Fortunately, I had a lot of help from the leadership at the Academy. The staff was there to help me, and I discovered they would meet me halfway. The professors and military instructors were always willing to tutor me, as long as I was willing to work. They would spot me some extra time to let me catch up when I missed classes for football.

Remember, when the Naval Academy goes to the trouble to admit us, they don't admit us to fail. They screen us so we can succeed. After that it's a matter of attitude. If you want to do it, they will help you get it done. You just have to request the help and then do what they ask you to do.

> *"The Academy taught me how to learn, how to ask questions, how to solve problems."*

I discovered that the more structure I had, the better I responded. If I had gone to a civilian college, and was completely responsible for myself, I probably would have been a five year student. But the struggle to deal with military requirements, academic requirements, and intercollegiate sports all at once forced me to compartmentalize and structure my time. So I really learned time management, a skill more valuable to me now than ever.

I also learned something I didn't really appreciate until later: a healthy appetite to want to know things. I think that desire gets stronger the older I get. The Academy taught me how to learn, how to ask questions, how to solve problems. I had no idea that's what I was learning.

I learned teamwork as well. When you play a team sport at the Naval Academy, you learn to be a good teammate against world class opponents. We played teams like Penn State, Notre Dame, and Michigan. Those were daunting challenges. But you learn how to come back from adversity—how to prevail when you're losing, and the importance of winning. In warfare specialties, we need that kind of competitiveness.

I learned that leadership is how to accomplish a mission, and how to become a tougher, more resilient person. These qualities kept me alive in a few situations. These qualities prepare our men and women to lead in combat.

Service academies are good at instilling these qualities in everyone, but athletics take it to an even finer level. It's something different to be battling it out in front of a crowd on national TV. That's why competitive athletes succeed in Navy SEAL training at a much higher rate.

My advice to high school athletes is that if you want to enter the Naval Academy because you want to be a naval officer, you will have a tremendous opportunity to compete on the national level. Don't go because you want to be a professional athlete; that's the wrong motivation. The Naval Academy is a means to an end: to take a commission as an officer.

If you play competitive sports, you must like a challenge, and attending a service academy is an extraordinary challenge. You can find a lot of institutions of higher learning where you can feel comfortable, but it's much harder to go where you know you will be uncomfortable. You need to want to be challenged, to really stretch yourself. If so, the Naval Academy has a lot to offer.

First Lieutenant Courtney O'Brien, Class of 2004. Lieutenant O'Brien played basketball at the Naval Academy before graduating and receiving a commission in the Marine Corps. She was selected to get a masters degree at the University of Maryland, then went to Marine Basic School at Quantico and flight school. She is now a KC-130J pilot.

I grew up near Gettysburg, Pennsylvania, and we often drove by the Naval Academy on the way to the beach. My dad would point it out. I knew it had a reputation as a great school. I was recruited by a lot of schools—Ivy League and other east coast schools—to play basketball, but the Naval Academy was the first college I visited.

I stayed with girls on the basketball team, and went to a Navy football game. Everyone seemed really disciplined and really focused. I knew I'd have a decent job for five years after I graduated, and a chance to see the world.[3] I knew I'd get a great education and a job that meant something, plus have the opportunity to play Division I athletics.

I didn't feel ready for Plebe Summer. There were people there who had wanted to go to the Naval Academy their entire life; they already knew *Reef Points* [military knowledge all plebes must memorize]. I was getting yelled at for the first time in my life, and I didn't know anything about rank structure or anything. But one thing I could do was keep up physically, excel athletically.

I had made my decision to go to the Academy in November of 1999, and I didn't realize how serious the decision was. After 9/11, a lot of us

---

3. Officers who attend flight school incur an eight year commitment after they get their wings, and for Lieutenant O'Brien (because of her time at graduate school) it took three years to get that far. So she is committed to serving for a minimum of 11 years. And she's perfectly fine with that.

realized this is for real now. I was really glad I was there and able to contribute, that I would have a job that mattered. All the training had a new sense of urgency; everything was for a reason.

At the beginning of the academic year, I was just convinced I was going to fail out. After getting to know my squad mates during the summer, how smart they were, I was sure I had the lowest SAT scores. I was convinced I got in on my basketball abilities alone.

So I established really good study habits right off the bat, and I actually did really well. I figured out the time management and balancing all the plebe duties, academics, and sports.

I had a really good relationship with my classmates, because I knew that I was a midshipman first and an athlete second. The guys in my company saw that I wasn't going to try to get out of anything. They came to a lot of our games.

The first time I went on a boat for a cruise, I decided I didn't want to be on a ship. But I had the chance to interact with a lot of Marine officers. I thought they were great; their character and leadership were unparalleled. On my cruise, there was a platoon of Marines, and they all volunteered to wash dishes or take out trash when they weren't busy. I really respected them all, and I knew that was what I wanted to be around.

> "What I learned in sports has definitely helped me in flight school."

So I decided to become a Marine aviator. I really enjoy the training. You can never get complacent. I really like that aspect.

What I learned in sports has definitely helped me in flight school. People who play varsity athletics learn so much more time management, and how to use all the resources available to them. At the Naval Academy, in my spare time over lunch, I lifted, went through plays, or shot baskets. After school we had practice from 3:15–6:30. Then I would eat dinner and be back in my room around 7:30. A lot of people had all afternoon free. We would often be gone on a trip from Thursday through Sunday, and missed a lot of classes. So I really learned how to prioritize and use my time wisely.

When we went on road trips, I was worried about how to learn what I missed or catch up on assignments. I found someone on the team or an officer who traveled with us to help me, or I called people from my class. I had to be creative to get the job done. I spent a lot of late nights on the bus reading, which is hard to do—after a loss it's hard to focus, and after a win you just want to celebrate.

But I took academics seriously. I would be thinking ahead and planning ahead, getting information from my professors before I left so I could stay on track. All the professors understand the demands placed on varsity athletes, and they're willing to spend the extra time with you.

You have to remember to keep a sense of humor, and know when it's time to be serious. Some days it might seem like it will never end, but you'll look back in the future and laugh and have some nostalgia. Everything that goes on during Plebe Summer has a reason and will pay off in the long run. I found I could get through all the information you have to learn in flight school much faster because of the memorization required during plebe year.

The Naval Academy is more of a commitment than if you went to a normal college, but it's worth it in the long run. You get an opportunity to serve your country and do something much bigger than yourself.

Midshipman First Class Zerbin Singleton, Class of 2008. Midshipman Singleton earned an appointment to the Naval Academy class of 2007, but broke his collar bone in a car accident and was deemed medically ineligible to attend. After attending Georgia Tech for a year, he entered with the class of 2008 and played running back for the Navy football team. He humbly sidesteps the challenges he faced in a difficult childhood, instead focusing on the service to country that lies ahead. He plans to become a Marine aviator after graduation.

Zerbin Singleton USNA PHOTO LAB

A counselor had told me about the Air Force Academy. I wanted to play Division I football, get a degree in aeronautical engineering, then fly. I was in Navy ROTC, and I applied to both the Air Force Academy and the Naval Academy. I liked the atmosphere better here.

Plebe summer wasn't tough physically. Mentally, it was a bit of an adjustment. I had been at a civilian college where I had lots of freedom, but I'm not a quitter. I got cut from Georgia Tech's football team. Here, I made the team as a walk-on before the summer was over. When you compare the practices, Georgia Tech was more laid back. And here, the coaches care about the individual. It's not just a business.

The academic year is hard because of all the things you have to balance. I don't get done with meetings or practice until 7:30. So I try not to sleep during the day, and stay away from the computer.

A few years back, the football team had a bad reputation, and they were considered lazy. But in reality they work four times as hard as everyone else. There's more at stake. There's no black flag for football practice [a caution sign that ends outdoor physical training when the heat and humidity are dangerously high]. I also try to lead by example—taking leadership responsibilities in the summer, maintaining a good uniform—and give the football team a good reputation.

If you come to the Naval Academy, be dedicated and motivated. Understand that you will be serving in the military. You will have lows, but the benefits outweigh them. You have to have a good attitude. Remember you're "only facing what other men have met."

Only facing what other men have met. Pretty wise words from a 23 year old. Besides being smart and talented and hard-working, Midshipman Singleton—and every other athlete I talked to, whether midshipman or graduate—all had a strength of character and evident leadership ability that was impossible to miss.

So I will conclude this chapter with these words of advice: If you want to stand out, to be seen as exceptional, known by all as the best of the best...maybe you SHOULDN'T go to the Naval Academy. You will be surrounded by people who are just as good, or better, than you.

But if you want to surround yourself with great people who will challenge you every day to be your best, if you want to serve your country alongside dedicated and talented leaders, the Naval Academy will provide you opportunities you cannot find anywhere else—and lessons that will serve you well throughout your life.

TWENTY
Frank Talk With A Minority Graduate

Lt. Bobby Jones.   USNA Photo Lab

This interview was conducted with Lieutenant Bobby Jones, class of 2001. Lieutenant Jones is a surface warfare officer and a diversity admissions counselor for the Naval Academy.

SR: *Tell me about your background.*

Lt. Jones: I grew up in Atlanta and went to a private school, where I was one of only 15 African-Americans in a class of 200. I came from a military family. I had uncles who served in the Marine Corps and the Army, but none were officers.

SR: *Why did you decide to go to the Naval Academy?*

Lt. Jones: I had seen David Robinson play basketball, and I said to my mom, "I didn't know the Navy had a basketball team." She told me it was a school, and I could go there—I just had to be good enough. I really wanted to do something that was very different from other college experiences. I was recruited by a lot of schools for football—I had many scholarship offers from Division I and Ivy League schools. But I also did well academically.

Serving in the military was a big deal to me. Being an officer, the first in my family, appealed to me. I applied to both Navy and Air Force, but I chose Navy. I'm a big history buff, and I knew it wasn't until 1949 that there was a black graduate from the Naval Academy; the first black naval officer was in 1944. Traditionally in the naval service, because of the rank structure, African-Americans had been shut out. I thought about that long and hard before I decided to attend the Academy.

SR: *What were the biggest challenges for you?*

Lt. Jones: The academies were honest with me about how difficult it would be. I checked in on July 1st and I wanted to go home on July 2nd. But I stuck through it, and I'm glad I did.

I was not the academic stalwart of the class. I was on academic probation all eight semesters, and I graduated dead last in my class. But I graduated—with a political science degree. The Academy will teach you how you best learn. A lot of intelligent people don't know how to study or how to learn.

One thing the Academy did for me was ensure I failed at something. I've learned that truly successful people know how to recover from failure. All academies have that lesson in common. I didn't like swimming, and they threw me in the water anyway. I didn't really like math or science, but there I was at one of the top five engineering schools in the country.

My self esteem was absolutely shattered, but I found out I could do more than I ever thought. Some people don't want to know their limitations, but in the end you're better off for it. I can't remember what I learned in electrical engineering, but I can tell you how hard I worked to get through.

SR: How were race relations in the Brigade?

Lt. Jones: I thought it was better than in society in general. People sometimes think of the military as conservative, but historically the military has been a forerunner in race relations. The military integrated long before society did.

Don't get me wrong, there's always one or two idiots [who are racist]. But stereotypes are quickly broken in this type of environment. For example, people see me and assume since I'm an African-American, I probably like rap and hip hop. What they didn't know is that I was an all-state band member, I played the tuba, and like classical music. My roommate was a white male from wine country in California. He never got to know anyone black before me. He learned a lot about my life and vice versa.

The Academy is a place where you get ahead on merit. Some of the mids said women shouldn't be here. But I laughed when I saw how physically qualified and smart they were.

Even though I did play football and ran track, I didn't come to the Academy for sports. I was a mid first. Football players were sometimes looked at as slackers, but after they graduate they seem to be the ones who get the awards and achieve great things. You learn that you can't judge a book by its cover. By the time you leave after fours years you get that message.

I tell minority kids that the Naval Academy minority population is low, but in any corporate boardroom, you will probably be the only one of color. You should not let race, color, ethnicity, or religion affect where you go.

SR: Talk about your experience in the fleet.

Lt. Jones: After graduation I served on the *USS Germantown* in Sasebo, Japan as the deck division officer. I helped conduct landings in Philippines for Operation ENDURING FREEDOM. Then I was the fire control officer on an Aegis cruiser. When I was finishing that tour, I got a call from the Naval Academy saying they wanted me to be a diversity admissions counselor. I said, "Have you seen my transcript?!"

One of the reasons I'm staying in the Navy is because there are so few minority officers in fleet, especially in senior ranks. A lot of that is because we have a different experience in the ward room. You just don't feel as comfortable because you're one of a few minorities. I was the most senior person of color on my ship as a lieutenant junior grade![1] The Navy is trying to fix that [increase the number of black officers], but it's going to take time.

Everyone who is a minority, either by race or gender, has some negative incident they can mention. But for the most part, when you work with people, you don't really focus on race issues. You have to trust the system that you will be judged on performance and ability, and not what you look like. If you work hard and put in the time, your people will see that, the leadership will see that, and give you credit. And I tell people that you can't underperform and expect to be treated well. You have to pull your own weight. Everyone has to prove themselves.

SR: *What is the biggest challenge in recruiting minority midshipmen?*

Lt. Jones: There are actually two. The first is one that every university in America is trying to deal with. African-Americans and Latinos are graduating from high school at a 50% rate, so we're competing for a shrinking talent pool. Many have been told that the way out of the ghetto is sports, so these kids don't stress academics and as a result aren't prepared to go to an institution with high academic standards.

Two: the military turns a lot of kids off. In the inner city, the African-American student says, "Why should I go serve in the Army [or another service] when I'm not yet a full-fledged citizen? Why should I work for a government that doesn't care about me?" But I tell kids, in order to change the system you have to be part of it. You need the credibility to go in and do something about it.

Sometimes kids look at the structure and discipline at the Academy not as an asset but as a hindrance. A few will respond positively, but we have to compete for them. If a minority is qualified to come here, then Harvard, Yale, Princeton, and Stanford are beating at their door as well.

Another challenge is parents. Seven times out of ten they're against the military. They think recruiters are coming to take their kids to fight this war. Many times there is only one parent, someone who didn't go to college, and they have no idea how the college application process works.

SR: *What advice would you give a high school student considering the Academy?*

---

1. A lieutenant junior grade is the second officer rank, after ensign, and typically has been an officer for two to four years. LT JG is equivalent to a first lieutenant in the Marine Corps, Army, or Air Force.

Lt. Jones: My own sister once asked me "Why should we send our best and brightest to a service academy when they can go to Harvard or Princeton?"

Here's my answer: For a couple of generations we have sent our best and brightest to those schools and they've done well. But the rest of society is still suffering.

What's missing is leadership. You can get a great education at an Ivy League school, but at the Naval Academy I can guarantee you will also learn leadership. You can then go back and motivate other kids to do more with their lives. You can have an impact on your community. You can look after other people besides yourself. Leadership: that's what is taught here and not at Harvard. It's a no-brainer to me.

SR: Any other advice?

Lt. Jones: Take the SAT early, starting your freshman year, twice a year. Not the PSAT, the SAT. Your scores are going to go up every time you take it because you will get more comfortable. Particularly in black communities, kids will wait until their senior year. I say, "You're going to take a test that will dictate the rest of your life and only do it once? That doesn't make any sense."

I took it in 7th grade for first time and I was the only kid in the room who wasn't a 12th grader. A basketball player will shoot three-point jump shots all day to get comfortable. So why would you take the SAT once?

Also, some American high schools tell you that you only need three years of math. Take four. I don't care if you're applying to a service academy or Harvard. They are going to look at your math score first.

Be athletic. The XBOX 360 generation is one of the softest we've ever produced. We've had kids come to Summer Seminar who couldn't do a single sit-up. Some can't run a mile, and don't even ask about pull-ups. Big soft-bodied kids say they want to be a Navy SEAL. That's not going to happen. You have to be able to lead from the front. We do a good job letting appointees know what's expected [physically] and that's paying off. The last plebe class [2011] came very well prepared as a result.

SR: What is your advice for surviving as a mid?

Lt. Jones: Check your ego at the door, especially minority kids. If you're qualified to come there, you've been told you're greatest thing since sliced bread, and you're probably number one at your school. Many minority mids are very independent because that was only way to get out of the situation they were in. Then they come here and they're told to follow and be part of a team. The adjustment can be difficult.

Remember that people are here to help you. You just have to listen and do what you're told. You can't cop an attitude; you have to follow the rules.

Because of the way you look [being a minority], if you do mess up it will be more noticeable. But all the rules are delineated for you—it's pretty simple. We don't want to just bring you here—we want you to graduate. The Academy will not give up on you unless you give up on yourself.

SR: Closing thoughts?

Lt. Jones: Recently I went back to Atlanta for my ten year high school reunion. I was comparing stories with lawyers and doctors. They were talking about how hard law school and medical school were. Our experiences were just totally different. We have the opportunity to shape the course of human events. I had been in East Timor, and the captain called me to his cabin and told me he was sending me ashore with the Special Forces team. I asked why, and he said, "You played Navy football. I know you can handle it."

There's a good reason why service academy graduates are so desirable when they get out of the military. As a young officer, you're going to be telling people old enough to be your mom or dad what to do. You're going to be operating multi-million dollar equipment. As a graduate of the Naval Academy, you have a reputation for success that precedes you. That legacy is all over the place, and that's something I wanted to be a part of.

LT Jones is married to a graduate of the Class of 2003. He jokes that the Academy gave him everything he needs in life, including a wife! He will soon leave the Naval Academy for department head school, then become a weapons officer on the *USS Mahan*.

TWENTY-ONE
Survival Advice For Women

Since the last edition of this book was published, there seems to have been a "sea change," a change in the overall environment for women at the Naval Academy. The most obvious change is in the numbers—women now comprise about 20% of the Brigade.

Women have been part of the Naval Academy for a full generation, and based on recent interviews, time has improved gender relations. When asked what special challenges women face or what specific survival advice they would need, almost all of the midshipmen, graduates, and BGOs interviewed had to stop and think for awhile. Then they described an environment that judged men and women equally, based on their achievements and merit, not their gender. They mainly offered advice that applies equally to men and women midshipmen.

As a woman midshipman, you will still stand out in the crowd a bit more than the men—which at the Academy is not always a good thing. Your mistakes may be more obvious than those of your male counterparts. You will have fewer choices when it comes to picking roommates. You will have to adjust your appearance to conform to the uniform standards—everything from clothes to make-up to hairstyle and jewelry will be strictly regulated.

But that does not mean you cannot be feminine and a good midshipman at the same time. The climate you will face will likely be positive, and your Academy experience will be almost identical to that of your male classmates. And most women midshipmen feel they are fully accepted by their male classmates.

This sea change may have something to do with changes across the Navy, where women can now serve in virtually every specialty.[1] Women fly fighters, serve on aircraft carriers, and deploy into combat zones.

Two women were interviewed for this chapter. One graduated over two decades ago. She has seen the operational Navy, and now supervises midshipmen. She has looked back on her own experiences, and watched how men and women in the Brigade get along today.

The second is a senior who holds a high-ranking position within the Brigade. She knows what being a successful woman in the Brigade is like from the inside.

Here is what they had to say:

---

1. As of this writing, women are barred only from submarines and special forces in the Navy. Because of their mission, the Marine Corps has more limitations.

Commander Anne (Groves) Hammond, Class of 1986

Commander Hammond was a varsity swimmer for Navy, and graduated as a math major. Her initial career field, called "General Unrestricted Line," performed human resources and training throughout the Navy. She is now serving in the Human Resources community. She has also served as a flag lieutenant as well as a recruiter. She is now a Battalion Officer at the Naval Academy, overseeing five companies of about 150 midshipmen each. She was recently selected for promotion to captain.

Commander Anne Hammond

ANNE HAMMOND

I grew up in Charleston, South Carolina, and attended a private prep school. A counselor thought the Naval Academy would be a good fit for me, but I had never even heard of it before. So my dad brought me up for a visit one weekend, and I went to class with a female mid, and then went to a football game.

I was sold. I don't know what it was about the place, everything I saw...I just knew it was what I wanted to do. Since I was a swimmer, I got in touch with the swim coach, who was very encouraging. I applied and I got accepted.

I'm not sure when it was exactly that I focused on the fact that I would be serving in the Navy when I graduated—I really didn't look beyond those four years at USNA until later on. But I definitely knew all along that I would get a great education and would have the chance to compete in swimming. I'm not someone who had always wanted to serve, and I was the first person in my family to be in the military.

I remember Plebe Summer being very difficult. I was in really great shape, but as a swimmer, I hadn't run a lot. I got shin splints from all the running. They issued us really bad athletic shoes back then. Now the plebes can bring their own running shoes, all broken in.

Mostly I remember it being very hot and we were sweating all the time, but Plebe Summer was fun at the same time, especially getting to know the other plebes. But we were also tired all the time. As a plebe, you're constantly at the pointy end of the focus of one or another upperclassman, yelling at you, getting you to learn a million things seemingly all at once.

As a woman, I thought I was always considered by my male classmates to be part of the company. I believe the other women in our company felt the same way too. We had an especially tight bond with the male classmates in our company. We were just one big group trying to get through the Naval Academy experience together. I do, however, know that women's experiences differed from company to company in that regard.

Now, one of every five midshipmen is a woman, and everyone here is very familiar with having women as integral members of the Brigade of Midshipmen. I think women mids are well accepted because they have proven that they can do all the work equally well and be successful in every aspect of their midshipman career. Early in the 1980s when women were being integrated into the Naval Academy, women were not so readily accepted throughout the Brigade as a whole. When I was here, I do think there might have been some perception from the males that women were being pushed into leadership positions they hadn't necessarily earned or didn't deserve. In my opinion, however, the women in my class who were in striper (leadership) positions all earned it.[2]

The first academic year was a bit of a shock for me. I had taken AP calculus, and I validated one semester of calculus, so I felt like I had an advantage. I did pretty well in high school, a prep school that was pretty challenging. But with the academic demands in addition to all the other demands at the Naval Academy, I didn't have all the proper study skills I needed. I'm amazed at how much the Academy does now to help the mids gain those skills—group studies, tools, tutors. All that wasn't in place back then.

> *"When I graduated, the career opportunities for women were much more limited than they are now."*

I did develop a very tight bond with the other women mids in our company, and that provided a good support mechanism. Being a member of a varsity team provided another very good support group, and the coaches were good sounding boards when times got tough. In general, all the athletics we were required to do helped us to maintain good physical fitness but also provided a very good stress reliever. When times were tough, there also was a chaplain network at the Academy—when I was a mid, they would walk around in the evenings and see how we were doing. I loved talking to them. Now we have a chaplain assigned to every battalion. It's helpful for the mids to be able to talk to people who aren't as involved in the mids' day-to-day life, people who can be more objective and give a different perspective.

When I graduated, the career opportunities for women were much more limited than they are now. Women couldn't serve in any combat-related specialties, and I wasn't able to select aviation due to my eyesight. So my

---

2. "Striper" positions, named for the extra stripes worn on the uniform, are leadership positions that rotate among the high-achieving midshipmen.

first assignment was to a training command in San Diego. I really enjoyed serving as a flag lieutenant on a combat logistics group staff in Norfolk, Virginia,[3] which at the time was responsible for the majority of East Coast ships that had women assigned.

My other favorite tour was in recruiting, in Albuquerque, New Mexico. I did four years—it was supposed to be a three year tour, but I extended a year. I think the main reason I enjoyed it was the interaction with people; in recruiting, you could see the results of your hard work immediately—when you were able to help people make a choice about joining the Navy or finding another options that suited them better.

In my experience, gender issues have not been much of a problem. Maybe I've been lucky, but I never felt personally discriminated against. I never felt I didn't have an opportunity to do something because I was a woman.

The biggest lesson I learned at the Naval Academy was prioritizing my time. Some things had to drop off the plate—you have to figure out what's the most important thing. Maybe in high school you always were striving for perfection and gave 110 percent, but I had to learn that I might only have time to complete an assignment with 90 percent effort. You have to work harder and faster, and be satisfied with a job done well, although not necessarily to perfection.

> *"The biggest lesson I learned at the Naval Academy was prioritizing my time."*

I also learned a very strong work ethic. I had to work very hard to make it through the Academy. That showed me that no matter hard something is, you can make it through by working hard. My four years as a mid engrained in me the commitment to do the right thing, whether it's because of abiding by the honor concept or just learning to do the right thing even if it isn't popular or easy.

Because of my academic struggles, my class standing at graduation was not very high, and as a result, I believe I had lower expectations (than some of my classmates) for the future with respect to my career. I didn't expect to be a superstar. As I reflect back in hindsight, I think that attitude actually helped me out. I went into each job to work hard and do my best, and then doors just seemed to keep opening for the next opportunity. My tours in the Navy kept being fun and now, all these years later, I am still on active duty and have just been selected for captain.[4]

---

3. A flag lieutenant is like an aide-de-camp, or personal assistant, for an admiral. Flag lieutenants help manage the admiral's schedule and also perform ceremonial functions.
4. Captain is the highest rank a Navy officer attains before becoming a rear admiral, equivalent to a full colonel in other services.

My advice to anyone who wants to come here is to start your preparation early, and get serious, especially where your grades are concerned. Also, do something athletic every day—play soccer, play pickup ball, something. If you come here, you will do something athletic every day, so you have to be used to that. You can also benefit from joining Junior ROTC or other organizations like Sea Cadets where you can get exposed to the military, Navy or otherwise, and learn how to wear a uniform.

My advice for women plebes, for anyone, is to be in best physical shape you can be in when you show up. Also, maintain your sense of humor and try not to highlight or bring attention to yourself, good or bad. Remember the training you will go through is all part of a process—it's not personal. Much of the goal is about helping each other get through the training as a unit, as a team—it's not all about you. Be part of the team, not someone who's doing things for yourself or dragging everyone else down.

The Naval Academy is a good place for women. There are tremendous opportunities for professional and personal experiences in so many areas. If you have a desire for military service, and also to get a jump start for whatever you want to do in life, the Naval Academy is a place you should consider.

In addition to the four years at the academy, you'll graduate and have to serve in the military typically for five to seven years. That probably seems like a long time. But it's nothing to get the right start in life. The job skills and leadership skills you get are incredibly valuable out there in corporate America. In the Navy, you be doing the same level of work as your male counterparts; you'll do the exact same things right after graduation as the men. I don't know whether or not that's true in the corporate world. I do know that women are definitely equals with their male counterparts in the Navy.

Show up in the best physical shape possible.
USNA PHOTO LAB

Midshipman First Class Erica Reid-Dixon, Class of 2008

Midshipman Reid-Dixon grew up in a military family and lived overseas for a number of years—both her parents served in the Air Force. She graduated from high school in Delaware. She was selected to be a "striper," and at the time of this interview held a leadership position as Brigade Chief of Staff. After graduating from the Naval Academy, she will serve in the Navy as a Surface Warfare Officer.

Midshipman Erica Reid-Dixon.
USNA Photo Lab

I just stumbled onto the Naval Academy. I went to an FBI leadership program the summer after my sophomore year in high school, and I was looking for something similar for the following summer. I wanted to be around the same kind of exciting program, so I went on line and Googled "summer leadership program." That's how I found the Naval Academy's Summer Seminar. Since it was only $300 and an hour away, I decided to go.

When I got to Summer Seminar, I had no idea what I was getting into. I saw the agenda and said, "We're working out?" But by the end of the week, I realized the Naval Academy was where I wanted to go. At the FBI leadership program, I thought, "There should be a school for people like this—driven people with great attributes and goals." This is that school. It's an environment where I can learn from the great people around me. So I jumped on the application, and finished it in two weeks.

I was so excited to come here. I found a web site where some midshipmen had posted some common rates you should know. One of them was the articles of the Code of Conduct. That's what I knew when I showed up for I-day, and I thought I was doing pretty well. Then I realized there's a whole book called *Reef Points* I would have to learn!

Plebe Summer I realized I could do so many things I would have never done if I hadn't come here, like shooting a rifle and a pistol and learning to sail—I had never sailed before in my life. I climbed a rope for the first time, and I did a lot of things I didn't realize I could do. That ingrains in you that you never know how far you can go until someone pushes you. Plebe Summer was definitely tough. I got on the wrong side of one of my cadre, but it made me a better person because I learned not to judge people by what other people say. Second detail was a fresh start.[5] Despite the challenges, I remembered to laugh and have fun.

---

5. The upperclass cadre swaps out for the second half of Plebe Summer.

I came to the Academy in good physical shape. During Summer Seminar, I completely failed the PRT, so I had a gauge of what would be expected. I didn't want to be the "load," the last girl, the one who was falling out during runs or finishing last all the time. I didn't want to just meet the standards, I wanted to exceed them. So the physical aspect wasn't much of an issue for me. There is always going to be that person who hasn't done anything to get in shape, and takes awhile to get caught up. Plebe Summer is that much harder for them.

I don't think there were any gender issues during Plebe Summer—it's an individual thing. There are always going to be people who don't believe women should be here, and that could manifest in subtle or obvious ways. But personally, I haven't experienced anything that I could say is a gender issue. As women are put in leadership billets, and doing their job and doing it well, those issues fall by the wayside. There are enough people to check them [people who may be prejudiced against women].

Academically, I was one of the people who should have gone to NAPS. I finished my application early, and I got a letter of assurance to NAPS, but I kept pushing. I kept sending any update I could. I told them when I took a college course or competed in competitions. Eventually I got in [to the Academy].

We took a lot of academic placement tests the first few days. Based on my SAT scores and those tests, I was put in a remedial math program. So I had a built-in study period with a professor, and it really did help. I asked questions and we went over tests. If you're willing to put the effort forth, you can do it. The Academy will help you. Statistically, I shouldn't have done as well academically as I did! Chemistry was a killer, and I got a "D." But I worked really hard for that D—D for done.

As a woman midshipman, it's really important that you set the tone. You have to say, "I'm a strong woman; this is what I'm good at, and this is what I need help with." How you interact with your classmates, how you handle situations, will determine how the next three years will go. Stuff will stick with you. You really have to think about the decisions you make.

It's not like a regular college. You're not just dating and having a good time [with your classmates]; you're going to be working together. You don't get to go home at the end of the day. The line between your personal life and your job is always blurred. Your personal decisions have to be those you aren't going to regret professionally. If you make mistakes like getting involved with an upperclassman or dating within your company, it can really jeopardize your credibility.[6] Mistakes will stick with you. You can't mix personal and professional relationships.

---

6. Plebes are not allowed to date other mids. Upperclassmen can date, but not within their company or chain of command. Some of the male midshipmen frown on those who date female midshipmen, calling it "Dark-siding."

I was really, really fortunate that I had a great group of girls in my company. In some companies the women are really tight, and some are cliquey and don't get along. But you have to learn not to judge people by what you hear about them. You have to take the time to get to know one another. This place is like one big locker room—you have to keep that in mind as a woman. You have to stay close and not turn on each other. If you don't get along with the women in your company, then reach out for friends somewhere else. It's important to have that avenue.

Anytime you go out for any sort of leadership position, people are always going to try to find something wrong with you, whether you are male or female. But you prove yourself. There are perceptions of stripers in general, not related to gender, that we're universally uptight.

I think it's a misconception that you have to absolve yourself of all femininity if you come to the Academy. There are a lot of extremely attractive women here who have been able to maintain their femininity. Women mids don't usually wear makeup to class because they just roll out of bed and get going. Then on the weekends, it's a blowout. Many will get really dressed up, and go all out with their hair and makeup.

"...it's a misconception that you have to absolve yourself of all femininity if you come to the Academy."

After graduation, I hope to get a port in Japan. I've heard that your reputation at the Academy actually continues after graduation. Back to those decisions you make here...they can follow you out into the fleet. You have to remember that you will be working with these people [other mids] when you get in the fleet, and you don't want to be constantly battling rumors.

You also have to be aware of the tone that you set when you get there [to your active duty unit] and the rapport you build with people, men and women. I've heard that from officers as well. Someone in your unit might try to proposition you, but you have to put a stop to it right away.

My final words of advice: Always know yourself. Plebe Summer, there are people who are going to be making assumptions and judgments about you. If your pencils aren't lined up correctly, they'll say you are going to be a bad officer. You have to say, "I know I came here for a reason," and be confident and stick with it.

If you are a woman considering the Naval Academy, you should find a woman midshipman or graduate and talk to her yourself. Find out first-hand about her experiences and advice. Then compare what she tells you to the interviews in this chapter. If you decide that the Naval Academy offers you opportunities you can find nowhere else, then follow the advice of Midshipman Reid-Dixon: "Be confident and stick with it."

TWENTY-TWO
You Must Live By The Honor Concept

Much of this section talks about how to get along with other midshipmen. The subject of this chapter is how you must live with yourself.

Specifically, you must live honorably, both as a midshipman and later, as a naval officer.

Consider the following scenario: Two plebes, tired and overworked and frustrated, get their hands on the latest DVD, a comedy that everyone is talking about. So they decide to take a study break and pop it into the computer. After watching it for about a half an hour, they hear upperclassmen in the hall and decide to hide the DVD because they are not allowed to watch movies in their room. A few minutes later, an upperclassman knocks on their door and asks one of the plebes, "Are you watching movies in here?" They will be in trouble if they are caught, and the movie has been turned off. So the plebe answers, "No, sir!"

He has just violated the Naval Academy's Honor Concept.

THE HONOR CONCEPT

The words of the Academy Honor Concept provide a prescription for your personal behavior:

Midshipmen are persons of integrity: They stand for that which is right.

a.   They tell the truth and ensure that the full truth is known. They do not lie.

b.   They embrace fairness in all actions. They ensure that work submitted as their own is their own, and that assistance received from any source is authorized and properly documented. They do not cheat.

c.   They respect the property of others and ensure that others are able to benefit from the use of their own property. They do not steal.

But the Honor Concept is an idea that is broader and more positive. Without honor there is no trust, and without trust there can be no teamwork.

A part of the idea is how midshipmen are to be treated by their classmates, faculty, staff and officers. It will always be assumed that midshipmen are honorable. They can be trusted at all times. They are forthright under all circumstances. They are people who, if they say they will do something, they will do it because giving their word is the same as pledging their honor.

Another part of the idea is how midshipmen relate to others. Specifically, midshipmen must always be ready to judge honorable and dishonorable behavior when they see it around them. They must neither permit behavior of the dishonorable type, nor accept anything that results from dishonorable behavior. In other words, living with the Honor Concept requires midshipmen to take on the responsibility of seeing that everyone else also lives by it.

This requires midshipmen to take action whenever they believe they have observed dishonorable behavior. That action may take one of three different forms.

1. Midshipmen may confront the offender and informally counsel the person. This option is called "confront and discuss."
2. Midshipmen may confront the offender and get more facts, including the offender's side of the story, then report the incident. This is the "confront, discuss and report" option.
3. Midshipmen may report the incident directly to the Midshipman Honor Organization. In Academy jargon, this is the "report" option.

What if a midshipman observes an offense and does nothing?

Doing nothing is also an offense. However, it is considered a failure of leadership, rather than an "honor" offense, which could result in separation (being permanently expelled).

WHAT HAPPENS TO MIDSHIPMEN WHO LIE, CHEAT, OR STEAL?

And what happens to those who have been turned in for an honor violation?

Their cases are entirely in the hands of the Brigade Honor Organization, which is administered by the midshipmen.

When a potential violation has been reported, the midshipman chain of command does a preliminary investigation to find out the facts. If the accused midshipman admits to the offense, then the case goes to a hearing for "sanction and remediation."

Who conducts the hearing? It depends on the infraction. For example, a plebe who commits a first offense that is not premeditated will probably have a hearing with the midshipman company commander. Take the example at the beginning of this chapter: the plebe who answers without thinking. If he immediately admits he lied, and he had not been in trouble before, his case would be handled at a low level. For a first classman with a previous honor offense, a higher ranking midshipman—probably a regimental commander—would preside over the hearing.

What if the accused midshipman says he or she is not guilty? Then a more formal investigation begins. If the investigation warrants, the case will go to an honor board, consisting of a "jury" of nine midshipmen, plus a presiding officer who acts as an advisor. This honor board determines if the midshipman is in violation of the honor concept—guilty or not guilty in civilian terms. If the midshipman is found in violation, a hearing will determine the "remediations and sanctions."

What does sanction and remediation mean? Sanctions are punishments for the offense. A sanction may include restriction to the yard or loss of other privileges. Remediation is designed to help the midshipman learn from his or her mistake and resolve to make better decisions in the future. Remediation may include journaling, research papers, and time spent with a midshipman or officer mentor.

In the most egregious cases, the regimental commander may recommend the guilty midshipman be disenrolled from the Naval Academy. The officer chain of command, and ultimately the Secretary of the Navy, must approve this decision.

In the last year, about 20 midshipmen, less than 0.5% of the entire Academy, left because of honor violations.

LIVING UNDER THE HONOR CONCEPT

According to an officer who oversees the Honor Organization, the program has been changed recently to be more instructive, encourage midshipman involvement and speed up the process.

"If mids enter the Naval Academy from a high school where most students have cheated or seen others cheating, how do you develop and teach them if the only response to an honor violation is expulsion? We want them to have an opportunity to learn from their mistakes and get back on track—not zero tolerance.

"We were averaging about 100 cases per year, but we thought there would be more than that if people weren't hesitating to report out of loyalty to their classmates. We wanted to give them an opportunity to take action.

"So we added an opportunity for midshipmen, if they witness an offense, to speak with the individual and clarify it on their own. If they find out there really was no offense, there is no need to report it. If the individual is confronted and understands what they did was wrong, there is still no requirement to report it. But if the offense is serious, or the offender doesn't understand what they did was wrong, then the witnessing midshipman should report it."

Generally, midshipmen who were interviewed were strongly supportive of the Honor Concept. Most midshipmen take the concept of living honorably very seriously, and try very hard to do the right thing.

Several confessed coming from high schools where lying, cheating and stealing were common. They expressed relief to be out of that kind of environment and into one where there is complete mutual trust.

One graduate gives the following advice: "Place loyalty above everything…except honor." In other words, you may find yourself in a position where friendship and teamwork must come second to upholding the standards of the Honor Concept. Doing the right thing is not always easy.

Plebes can make it easier by looking around them and seeing how proud the upperclassmen are of living by those standards. The midshipmen

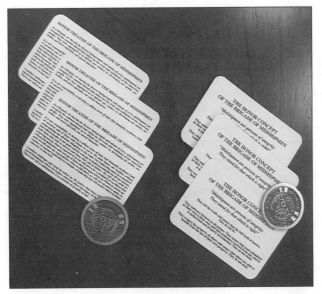

These coins and cards are tangible symbols of the Honor Concept.   USNA PHOTO LAB

who commented on the Honor Concept expressed nothing but pleasure in living with classmates who believed in living honorably.

Plebes get a number of lessons on honor and character during Plebe Summer. They will memorize the honor concept as a plebe rate, and watch an honor board or hearing. At the end of Plebe Summer, they receive an "honor coin" that links them to the class that graduated fifty years before theirs, and reminds them that the Honor Concept connects them to all other Naval Academy graduates. Midshipmen continue to discuss honor and moral leadership in professional training classes over the course of the next four years.

Midshipmen are asked to recommit themselves to the Honor Concept when they begin their second class year—the point where they have a binding commitment to serve for five years after graduation. Before they sign their commitment papers, they sign an honor scroll.

Most graduates report that the habit of being a person of integrity stays with them their entire lives, and anyone who is familiar with the Naval Academy knows that graduates can be trusted. This is a great advantage for grads who end up in the business world; it is a matter of life and death for those who serve together in combat.

TWENTY-THREE
Advice For Parents

Parents are always concerned when their sons and daughters leave home for college. Many worry about their safety and well-being in the new surroundings. Many others worry about how they are going to pay the ten to twenty thousand dollars the education is going to cost each year.

The parents of Naval Academy midshipmen do not have either of those worries. The Naval Academy is one of the safest places a young man or woman can be, and the education does not cost parents anything, at least for traditional college expenses.

That is the good news.

The bad news is that being a midshipman is much more demanding than being a regular college student. The demands on the parent are different as well. The demands include time, patience, some money and lots and lots of a hard-to-define commodity called moral support.

In short, Naval Academy parents have a unique role and it is important to the survival of their midshipman for them to learn what they should do. Equally important is learning what you should not do as a parent. Parents can actually hurt their children during the application process by doing too much of the wrong thing.

The role of the parent is what this chapter is about. To define it, more than seventy parents of Academy midshipmen or recent graduates were interviewed.

The parents were asked to describe the problems they and their midshipmen experienced from the time they became involved in the admissions process through the end of their midshipman's first year, or "plebe" year. It is by far the most difficult year for both the midshipmen and the parents.

The parents were also asked to use twenty-twenty hindsight and give advice on how to resolve the different problems they encountered—advice that could be passed on to the parents of candidates in this book.

In addition, numerous plebe midshipmen were asked to comment on parental support and the kinds of things that have helped them and their roommates. Officers and congressional staffers involved in the admissions process have advice for parents as well.

THE PROSPECTIVE CANDIDATE

Apply for the Right Reasons

During all the interviews one bit of advice was heard over and over, and it was strongly recommended that it should be the first advice parents of prospective candidates should hear: Make ABSOLUTELY SURE that going to the Naval Academy is your son or daughter's idea, not someone else's.

Nearly everyone had a story to tell about a young man or woman who went to the Academy because someone else wanted them to go. These stories never have a happy ending.

Typically, they end with the midshipman quitting, then going home to the emotional trauma of facing relatives, friends, and admirers who all believed he or she had a great opportunity but threw it away.

When asked to talk about their friends who quit, almost every midshipman had an answer similar to this fourth classman's: "We had one girl over the summer who quit. She was doing it [attending the Academy] for her parents, actually. That's what she told us. So it just didn't work out for her."

Another typical ending was for the midshipman to be expelled for poor academic or military performance. Often this is the face-saving tactic of a poorly motivated midshipman. He can then go home and say, "I tried, but I couldn't hack it."

As a parent, make sure you help your son or daughter examine their motives. Said one dad, who is also a Naval Academy graduate, "When my daughter first said she wanted to go to the Naval Academy, I discouraged her, because I thought she was doing it for me. But it became clear she wanted to do it for herself, so I threw my support behind her."

While interviewing parents, three different parents admitted, after their sons dropped out or were expelled, that they themselves were the real cause. The typical comment was: "He was really there for us. He knew we were so proud of him that he just kept plugging away until the system got to be too much for him." Make sure it is your son or daughter who wants to go to the Academy.

Another bit of advice is a logical extension of the preceding: Make sure that your son or daughter wants to go to the Academy for the right reasons.

According to many who evaluate colleges and universities, as well as many graduates and midshipmen, the Naval Academy offers an outstanding academic experience. But if that is all that your son or daughter wants, it would be a mistake to go there.

The goal of the Academy is to produce high quality naval officers. They will work long hours in the service of their country, and most will endure separations from their families on sea duty and deployments to austere locations. A high quality college education certainly lies at the heart of the Academy program, but a whole lot more goes along with it.

Many parents clubs host social events for appointees to get acquainted.

DANNY GERSTNER, LOUISIANA PARENTS AND ALUMNI CLUB

The Naval Academy education is above all a four-year officer training program. It is rigorous and demanding and requires young men and women to make great personal sacrifices, especially of their personal freedom. Prospective candidates should have firm goals that are in concert with the Academy's mission. If they want to become officers and serve their country in the military, after proving and improving themselves in a high-stress environment, then they stand a good chance of succeeding. It all depends upon how badly they want to achieve their goal.

However, if they are going for ANY other reason, or if their goal is not clear, perhaps you should suggest they look elsewhere. There are hundreds of high quality civilian colleges and universities where they can get an excellent education without enduring the rigors of the Academy. And they also will avoid the emotional trauma that comes from being branded as a quitter, or the guilt and feelings of failure that come with being expelled.

Know What They Are Getting Into

Another common story about midshipmen who quit is that they just did not realize what the Academy experience would be like. Parents are advised to do everything they can to enable a candidate to learn as much as possible about the Academy. The following is a variety of suggestions on how to achieve that goal.

Said one parent from Wisconsin, "My daughter went to Summer Seminar; that helped mentally prepare her. I was surprised that they really did do a mini Plebe Summer. They had them doing PT [physical training], and they were yelling at them. It's great to go to summer seminar, especially for a fence sitter, to rule it in or rule it out."

Summer seminar provides candidates with a taste of Naval Academy life, including academic, military, and physical training. Candidates can apply on line in February of their junior year at www.usna.edu/Admissions/nass.htm. A Summer Seminar application also counts as a preliminary application to the Naval Academy. The program is very competitive, offering about 1,800 slots for 6,000 applicants. Historically about a third of Summer Seminar attendees accept appointments to the Naval Academy.

An alternative, which is available anytime during a high school student's junior or senior year, is a tour and admissions briefing beginning at the Armel-Leftwich Visitors Center. Tours are available in the summer, but it is MUCH BETTER to go during the academic year when Academy life is at its normal high intensity.

A third alternative is to attend a sports camp. The Academy offers week-long programs in a variety of sports from football and basketball to rowing and swimming. You will have to fund the travel expenses and registration fees. While not specifically geared for potential candidates, the camps provide a chance to see the Academy up close. Schedules and registration information can be found at www.navysports.com.

One of the candidate's key supporters in the admissions process is the blue and gold officer. Blue and gold officers, or BGOs, are representatives of the Academy admissions office. There are more than 2,000 nationwide—every high school has a BGO. Many are Reserve officers, although some are still on active duty, some are counselors or educators, and some are parents of midshipmen or graduates. Many are Naval Academy graduates themselves. BGOs can answer questions about the admissions process, and they can help candidates get in touch with graduates or midshipman who can tell candidates what to expect if they get an appointment.

In addition, many areas of the country have active parents clubs, and their officers understand the importance of prospective candidates getting advice from midshipmen. They, too, will help arrange meetings.

The bottom line is that every option should be pursued to learn more about the Academy beforehand.

Prospective candidates must also have a realistic knowledge of what it means to be a military officer. Parents can help by locating an active duty or retired officer to discuss the many aspects of life in the Navy or Marine Corps.

WHAT ARE PARENTS' CLUBS?

Parents clubs provide a variety of services and support systems for midshipmen and their families. These include everything from social events to acquaint midshipmen and their families, to care-package stuffing parties. Some parents clubs host elaborate holiday celebrations. Many write letters or birthday cards to midshipmen.

Parents clubs also provide contacts and support for families. Parents may find it helpful to have other parents to talk to, parents who have survived their child's plebe year or the whole four years. They can tell you the do's and don't's of Plebe Parents Weekend, how to handle downer phone calls, or the latest news from the Academy. Most parents clubs have good web sites with pictures from the Academy, and information about upcoming events.

To find a parents club near you, visit www.usna-parents.org/clubs.html and click on your state.

THE ADMISSIONS PROCESS

Getting into the Naval Academy is a three-step process. Becoming a candidate is the first step. The student fills out a preliminary application on line in April of his or her junior year. If the student is qualified after this initial review, he or she becomes an official "candidate." Test scores, such as SATs, can be updated at any time in the process, so do not let your son or daughter delay filling out the preliminary application just because they are scheduled to take (or retake) the SAT in May or June.

Once they become a candidate, your son or daughter must get a nomination from someone eligible to give one. The most common nomination sources are the two U.S. Senators from the candidate's state and the U.S. Representative from the candidate's congressional district. A smaller number of nominations are awarded by the U.S. President, Vice-President and other sources that are described on the admissions web site. Most nominations are announced in late fall of the candidate's senior year.

The third step, after receiving a nomination, is to get an appointment to the Naval Academy. The appointment is a letter officially admitting the nominee and is awarded solely by the admissions officials of the Naval Academy. Contrary to what many parents will have heard, neither U.S. Senators or Representatives nor the U.S. President or Vice-President give appointments to the Naval Academy.

Also, parents should realize that not all candidates who are given nominations get appointments. For example, there are 535 U.S. Senators and Representatives and each one may nominate ten individuals for every vacancy. (Each senator and representative has a quota of five persons who can be at the Academy at any one time.) Thus, in a typical year, the senators and representatives alone can make at least 5,350 nominations. Yet, each year the Academy will only give about 1,300 appointments.

The entire process of getting a nomination and appointment is long and involved and is thoroughly explained for the candidate in earlier chapters. The purpose of discussing the subject in this chapter is to define the role of parents in the admissions process. What should they do and what should they not do?

Many parents believe that candidates need help with all the steps required.

Said a mother from New York: "These kids are under a lot of pressure during the last year of school—they are out for sports; they have leadership responsibilities and they are trying to maintain top grades. They can't always be well organized and that is where we can help. Also, the parent can keep track of all the deadlines for paperwork, appointments for interviews, physical and medical exams—and all the other little things. Kids can get messed up if the parent doesn't help them keep organized and it is real easy to miss a deadline."

However, parents are also cautioned not to get themselves completely involved in the paperwork. For example, they should not fill out the forms for the candidate, nor should they make calls to congressional offices or the Naval Academy asking questions about procedures.

...parents are also cautioned not to get themselves completely involved in the paperwork.

Why not?

Because everyone involved in the process of screening candidates is looking for those who are applying because of parental pressure. The survival record at the Academy is disastrous for midshipmen who have gone there because it was what their parents wanted. Unless midshipmen are totally committed by their personal desire to be at the Academy, they are almost certain to quit or get themselves expelled.

So, everyone involved in screening candidates is suspicious of any parental involvement in tasks that candidates could be doing for themselves. And because of the very intense competition between thousands of qualified candidates, there is a strong desire to nominate and appoint those who exhibit the strongest personal motivation.

And how motivated are candidates who cannot do their own paperwork or make their own telephone calls? Do not let that question be asked about your own son or daughter. Stay in the background. Help the candidate get organized, but stay out of the process yourself. Do not do anything that would make anyone question your son or daughter's motivation.

Besides helping candidates stay organized, there are other worthwhile things parents can do to help during the admissions process. First, support them if they want to take the SAT or ACT multiple times. Very often, their scores will improve as they become more familiar and comfortable with the test. The Academy will take their highest score, even taking the verbal score from one test and the math score from another if it works to the candidate's advantage. The time and money required to take the tests over and over are small investments for what could be a tremendous opportunity.

Parents may also need to get involved when the candidate hits a snag in the admissions process. For example, a father from Texas got involved when his son was turned down because of bad vision and because the boy had experienced some asthma when he was younger. That father's message to other parents was:

"Don't give up. We had our son's vision tested by our ophthalmologist and he found our son to be within the limits specified by the Academy. Even though he had already been turned down by the Academy, they accepted the letter from our ophthalmologist.

"His previous asthma was more of a problem but I eventually got them to agree to a pulmonary function test that he passed with no problem.

Parents may also need to get involved when the candidate hits a snag in the admissions process.

"I think a lot of parents would have a tendency to say, 'Oh well, there's nothing I can do when they are turned down. That's not true. I urge all parents to challenge the system if you believe the child is qualified."

A mother and father from Connecticut did not have medical problems with their son, but the story of their persistence and success might help some other parents:

"By the middle of April we hadn't heard anything and then we got this letter saying that our son was among 2,400 who were qualified. We asked around and found out that this was really a 'kiss-off' letter but my wife and son decided to go down to the Academy and talk to a friend who was there.

"He suggested that they talk to the head of the Naval Foundation who was very nice but said our son was not on his list of candidates for one of the prep schools. But he stressed the importance of showing commitment and suggested that we knock on some other doors. After that our friend hailed a professor from the math department who looked at our son's SAT scores and said they weren't bad at all. Then he started asking us about some of our son's other abilities. When he learned that our son was an excellent trumpet player and had played in a number of school musicals, he sent us to the music director. This man was very interested in our son, but he explained that he was not allowed to recruit. Yet he was very supportive and said he would make a few calls on our behalf."

Their son got in and the parents are not sure whether the music director's calls were helpful or not. But they believe that they were, and other parents with similar experiences stressed the importance of having an advocate at the Academy—someone there who really wants a candidate.

Parents should keep in mind that there are numerous minor sports at the Academy, and the coaches who recruit athletes may not know of a champion 128-pound wrestler from Buffalo, Wyoming or an all-conference cross-country runner from Marvell, Arkansas. Such a candidate, during a visit to the Academy, just might be able to convince a coach to become an advocate on his or her behalf. That is no guarantee of admission, but, according to parents who, through their own intelligence network have gained a lot of information about the Academy, a coach who is a strong advocate for a candidate can be very helpful.

Another good way for parents to help, without interfering, is to set up a practice interview with your son or daughter. All the mids who discussed the admission process recommended that candidates practice for the interviews with blue and gold officers and congressional staffers. You can do this yourself, using experiences from job interviews, or you can find a respected family friend to do it for you.

"If they make the offer, jump on it. I absolutely, strongly recommend it."

Parents should also realize that some candidates who are attractive to the Academy but who are borderline academically may be offered the option of attending a prep school for a year. The Naval Academy has a prep school of its own called NAPS. It is free to all those who are offered a year's preparatory study there. In addition, the Naval Academy Foundation has contracts with several private institutions around the country. They are not free; however, the Foundation has scholarships for needy students.

According to admissions officials and the Director of the Foundation, some candidates and their parents react negatively when the prep school option is offered.

That is a big mistake, according to midshipmen who elected that option and were interviewed. They said they were very glad they had taken the extra year and they felt they were much better able to tolerate the academic shock and hassles of the plebe year compared to those who came into the Academy right out of high school. Those from NAPS were also happy to have nearly 200 friends from their prep school class when they arrived at the Academy.

The parents who were interviewed were unanimous in their praise of the program and felt that the extra maturity gained by their sons and daughters made their Academy experience much more worthwhile. A father from Maine, who admitted being skeptical about the program initially, was asked what he would say about the program if a good friend called and asked his advice. He said:

"If they make the offer, jump on it. I absolutely, strongly recommend it. It is a great transition and it makes them a year older when they go. Instead of the double shock of being away from home and encountering the pressures of the Academy, they just have the Academy to stress them. But I would also tell a friend that he is inviting disaster if the kid really doesn't want it."

One final point about the admissions process was made by a Tennessee father who also is a blue and gold officer. He said:

"Warn parents that the Naval Academy is usually the slowest of the service academies to send out their appointments. I have lost some of my candidates because of this. They had applied at other academies and when they were notified of an appointment to one of them, they accepted immediately and then became ineligible for the Naval Academy appointment which came later. Advise parents to have the kids wait until the deadline for accepting the appointment for a second-choice academy—usually the deadline is around the first of May. That way they can have the backup and perhaps still get into the Naval Academy if that is their first choice."

PLEBE SUMMER

Help Your Plebe ...

Around the first of July the new appointees have to report to the Naval Academy for induction. The day they report, called I-Day, is a traumatic experience, both for the inductees and their parents if they accompany them.

Inductees find it traumatic because, in the words of a New Jersey mother: "They go there being told how wonderful they are; they have been at the top of their class; they had all the people at home telling them how proud they were of them; they get a wonderful send off; then within a span of two hours and a quick welcome aboard, they become dirt. They are treated like second-class citizens; their squad leader starts pushing them around; they put on a uniform that doesn't fit; they get all those shots and then their head is practically shaved."

And if the parents go along for that day, they spend their time trying to catch glimpses of their son or daughter until, late in the afternoon after the swearing in ceremony, the new plebes get to spend a few minutes with their parents before they disappear into Bancroft Hall and embark upon six weeks of rigorous training called Plebe Summer.

Should the parents accompany their sons and daughters on I-Day?

Most parents who have done that also recommend it for others, saying that it is a momentous occasion in the family's life and it is something that will mean a lot in future years. Advocates also felt that it is a way to tell sons and daughters that they have the complete support of the family.

Some of the other parents felt that it was not that important to go on I-Day. A few thought that it would be a nice thing to do if the family could afford the trip or if they were close enough so travel was no problem.

More negative was a California mother who has had two sons at the Academy and who has been co-president of a parents' club. She said, "My sons and others we have spoken with don't think parents should be there on I-Day. They felt that it was harder on the inductees. Also, the kids from this area all leave the day before in a group and they start making friends right away—and those friendships will help keep them going after the swearing in."

Another California parent said, "I have had two sons go there and in both cases we felt that it would be less stressful on them if they didn't have to think about us. Also, we felt that we could better use that travel money for a visit later in the year. Parents should also realize that Thornton Studios in Annapolis video tapes the I-Day proceedings and that they can see their son or daughter at least three times on tape—if arrangements are made ahead of time."

Many parents...stressed the importance of humor for the survival of the midshipmen.

There was absolutely no disagreement on what parents should do right after I-Day. Their admonitions can be summarized with three words: SUPPORT YOUR MID!

First and most important are the letters that you should write. Most parents said they tried to write something every day even if they had to strain to think of things to write about. Said a mother from Michigan, "Write even if it is only one page saying we had hamburgers for supper and the dog has been sleeping all day."

A mother from Minnesota agreed: "The important thing is to be regular with your writing. If you only write twice a week, that is okay as long as you keep it up because that kid will get used to expecting two letters a week. Just keep the routine going. And the letters don't have to be great and grand. Just tell what is happening at home. That is enough."

Many parents, especially the fathers who had also gone to the Naval Academy, stressed the importance of humor for the survival of the midshipmen. They say it is the humorous things that really keep the midshipmen's burdens from being oppressive.

Humor is also something that can be sent in from the outside by the parents. Several told of the hours they spent in stores shopping for funny cards that they could send. Said a mother from Virginia, "I shopped continuously and was able to send a different funny card for six weeks—all during Plebe Summer. He just loved them."

And said a mother from Maine, "I wrote a letter every day that whole first year and he said it really meant a lot to look in that mail box and know that something would be there. I clipped a lot of stuff out of the paper and I sent the Charlie Brown cartoon every day just so he would have a little laugh."

Some parents also mentioned some unique kinds of correspondence. Said a South Carolina mother, "Just before our daughter left that summer, I collected several books of quotations and started pulling out those that would be inspirational. Then I bought a six-month supply of postcards and copied a different quotation on each card. I sent one of those out each day and she really appreciated them. She shared them with her roommates and eventually I sent some to her roommates as well."

The most unique form of correspondence was described by a Florida mother: "Our daughter knew it was going to be very difficult and before she left she sat down and wrote 49 letters to herself. It was a big stack and she told me to mail one each day so she would get one during each day of Plebe Summer. I finally read one of them and it was very detached as though she was writing to another person. It said things like don't take it personally when they are screaming and yelling at you—it's something they have to do. Also that you have to keep your sense of humor and think how ridiculous they look screaming at you for things that don't matter. And this was all her idea. We had nothing to do with it."

Cough drops were recommended because the plebes have to yell a lot and are often hoarse.

Besides sending letters, almost every parent, and especially the midshipmen, strongly recommended sending care packages. Said a mother from Connecticut, "I sent a package every week with things like homemade cookies and brownies—also granola bars, nuts, trail mix and Kool-aid. We also sent cocoa mix, and various dried soups which they can make in their room because the water is so hot. They really need this extra nourishment during Plebe Summer."

Other parents recommended a variety of other things for the care packages. Cough drops were recommended because the plebes have to yell a lot and are often hoarse. Powdered drinks were recommended because the plebes are always dehydrated because of the high heat and strenuous exercise. Vitamins were recommended because of the inconsistent eating patterns that result from harassment during meals.

Several parents cautioned against making a fuss about a plebe's birthday during Plebe Summer. The rule for the plebes is never to draw attention to themselves, so do not give their detailers any excuse for picking them out of the crowd for special recognition.

One of the most frustrating things for parents is the difficulty they have communicating with the plebe by phone. At the Naval Academy parent telephone calls to the plebes are discouraged (except for emergencies, of course), and it is the rare parent who is going to see much written correspondence from their plebe. The reason for the latter problem is that the plebes simply do not have enough time to do everything they are supposed to do—and during what little spare time they might find, they are better off spending it getting a few moments of rest.

So what happens is that parents end up doing all, or practically all, of the letter writing and the plebes end up communicating with their parents by telephone. During Plebe Summer, a couple weeks may pass before they are allowed to make their first phone call.

So be prepared, say the parents who have been through it. Get your mid a telephone credit card, or get an 800-number the mid can use. The important thing is to make it as easy as possible for them after they have stood in line to use a phone.

And be ready for some hefty telephone bills, especially if the plebes are given a general purpose credit card and allowed to call their friends. Several parents recommended that they be allowed to do this, saying that they, the parents, are getting off cheaply not having to pay tuition and that such calls are great for boosting morale. Monthly phone bills of one-hundred to two-hundred fifty dollars are not uncommon, say the parents. (Plebes will probably not be allowed to have their cell phones with them during Plebe Summer, so we will save that topic for the next section.)

At the chapel, between services the chaplains have a social hour that plebes may attend.

For the parents who live close enough to drive to Annapolis on a weekend, it is possible to visit with your mid for about an hour on Sunday mornings. At the chapel, between the Catholic and Protestant services, the chaplains have a social hour that plebes may attend.

The parents who spoke about such visits expressed mixed feelings about them. Some felt that it was a wonderful opportunity to buck up the morale of the homesick mid. Others felt that such visits make it harder on the mid and that they negate one of the purposes of Plebe Summer, which is to cut the ties to mom and dad and shift the mids' dependence to their own support group—their peers.

Then there was the "Hey, Ralph!" story.

A father from New Jersey told about his and his wife's frustrations when their daughter went to the Academy. Not only were they lonely, but they wanted to support her. Yet, even though they lived relatively close, they knew they could not go there and visit her. But, then they came up with a bright idea. They checked with their daughter during a phone call. "Do you have anybody in your company named Ralph?" they asked. She said no. Shortly afterward they went to the Academy and observed the formations. Then, when they saw their daughter, the father yelled, "Way to go, Ralph! Hang in there, Ralph!" Said the father when he related this story, "This was great. She didn't dare show any expression—she had to look straight ahead. But you could see it in her eyes. She knew we were there and even though it was just a little thing, it meant a lot to her to know that we cared."

This story is related not to encourage parents to do the "Hey, Ralph" number, but to illustrate the type of creativity that parents use while trying to support their mid. The message that you want to communicate is, "We love you, kid, and we're 150 percent supportive of what you're trying to do."

The internet provides less intrusive ways to check on your plebe and find out what they are doing. The website for Parents of USNA Midshipmen is www.usna-parents.org. This site provides information about Plebe Summer, a parents' survival guide, contacts for parents clubs, and more.

Thornton Studios takes pictures throughout the summer, posts them (and sells them) on line. Their web address is www.plebesummer.com. Additionally, parents sometimes visit the yard and snap pictures, then post them on parents club sites. Many parents enjoy checking these pictures for a glimpse of their son or daughter.

... But Don't Hover

Now for the other side of the story.

Numerous parents, especially those involved in leadership roles in parents' clubs, as well as Academy officials, have told stories of parents who created problems for their mids—some of them severe. As an example of the latter, a senior official at the Academy told of two plebes who were interviewed as part of the dropout process. (Before plebes can leave, they must go through a series of interviews.) The official, with deep emotion showing on his face, explained that the two plebes had been told by their parents that they were being disowned for leaving the Academy. Luckily, one was going to live with a sister or brother, but the other young person left with no place to go.

The above cases are extreme, but not uncommon. Parents can become extremely emotional about the Academy, but the actions manifested from the emotions can go both ways. Equally as difficult, say those who work with the mids, are parents who cannot cut the parental cord with their mids. The author heard stories of mids, while struggling to keep their heads above water in Plebe Summer, receiving calls from mothers crying and telling their mids how desperately lonely it is at home without them. Everyone associated with those mids has said how demoralizing such phone calls are.

The irony of the latter problem is that it is often caused by otherwise excellent parents. Said a parents' club president, "The parents who cause those kinds of problems are wonderful people. They have been very involved in their kids' lives. They helped at the school and with extracurricular activities. They really care. But they can't cut loose. They still want to feel needed. But, they have to realize that they're going to have to suffer heartaches and hurt feelings—even anger. But that's the only way their mids are going to develop the independent traits they can be proud of on graduation day."

Part of the problem is with the Academy itself. The Superintendent greets parents who go to I-Day, and they are told, "If you have any problems, you be sure and call me—I'm here to help you and serve you." Typically, parents also get a letter from the mids' company officers giving them their phone number and telling them to call if they think there is a problem.

Well, some parents take them literally, and they call. Then the problems start when the information goes downhill through the chain of command—company officer to the senior who is company commander, then down to the upperclassman who is directly above the plebe. Of course, the last thing the plebe wants is to draw attention, and guess what dear mother or dear father has done to the plebe? The plebe now gets special attention!

There is also another aspect to this problem. The plebes cannot complain to their upperclass supervisors. Nor do they dare complain too much to their roommates—nobody wants to hear griping and moaning; it is too demoralizing. But many young people have been closely nurtured at home and need a crying towel from time to time while they are maturing and learning to become independent. Such young people need parents who will listen to their problems, but who will keep the communication within the family.

PLEBE PARENTS' WEEKEND

Toward the end of Plebe Summer, the Academy sets aside one weekend for a visit with parents. It is called Plebe Parents' Weekend, designed to give plebes and their parents a brief reunion. And of the advice given during all the interviews with parents, by far the strongest recommendations were aimed at convincing plebe parents that they should not miss this weekend. Here are some samples:

A father from Minnesota: "We were strongly encouraged to go but I thought it was rather silly to spend that much money. But, by the time the weekend was over, I realized it was definitely NOT silly. If there is any way in the world parents can go, I think they should. It is extremely important at this stage that they [the mids] know you are proud of them."

A father from Maine: "It is absolutely a must. I would come from Alaska if I had to. As a parent you owe it to yourself and you owe it to the

Everyone interviewed said MAKE SURE you go to Plebe Parents Weekend.

COULSON FAMILY

plebe. It is a real boost for them. They realize that they are not there alone [when the parents show up] and they need your support."

A father from New York and a graduate: "You just don't want to miss seeing that kid at that time. The transformation they have made is something to behold—you have to see it to believe it. They take that scruffy little kid on the fourth of July and by the middle of August the transformation is impossible to comprehend. You look at her and wonder if it is your kid. They mature so much in that time. They're very confident. I pride myself in being a good sailor, but when we went down I pulled out my old sailing card from my days and said, 'How about going sailing?' We took one of the knockabouts and she very quickly took charge and told me what to do and what I was doing right and wrong. I was speechless the whole time. I couldn't believe that this had happened in just a little over a month. She had learned not only to sail but to sail well."

A father from Connecticut: "Even if it's a sacrifice, you should go. They're not through Plebe Summer yet and they have a hard road ahead. They need that support. Also, the bond you build up that weekend will last the next fifty years because it is such an emotional experience. They work so hard for the week or two before that weekend to get themselves in shape for the parents. It's a milestone and if you absolutely cannot make it, arrange for a surrogate. Just don't leave the kid hanging there for the whole weekend. That would be a most horrible thing."

Are you convinced? If so, there is more that you should know.

For example, you must make your room reservations early. Annapolis is a busy place for tourists, not just parents. You are advised to make your reservations just as soon as your son or daughter has accepted an appointment. And do not forget, if grandfather and grandmother or other relatives will be going, they will also need rooms.

As of this writing, plebes are not allowed to spend the night away from the yard. It is recommended that parents stay as close to Annapolis as possible, so little time is wasted in traffic. And do not accept offers to stay with friends in the Washington, D. C. suburbs, even though a map makes the distance look minuscule. Along with the usual travel web sites, you can visit the county tourism site at www.visitannapolis.org to help you plan your visit.

Those who manage to get room reservations within walking distance of the Academy do not have to rent a car if they fly into Baltimore-Washington International—the airport of choice. There is a limousine that departs hourly that delivers passengers to the Annapolis motels. However, if you do decide to stay in Annapolis for the majority of the weekend, be prepared for long waits at crowded restaurants.

Also, you are strongly advised to take the opportunity to eat an evening meal in King Hall where all the mids eat. However, if you desire to do this, notify your mid so he or she can make reservations. Because there are so many parents, some have to dine there on Friday while others have to dine on Saturday. Some of the parents felt that, given a choice, Friday is better and that you should ask your mid to get reservations for that night.

Remember to have realistic expectations for the time you will spend together.

Many parents also want to do some sightseeing in Washington, D.C. while they are in the area. If that applies to you, it is recommended that you go early and get all the sightseeing out of your system before you greet your mid—or stay afterward and plan on sightseeing later. The Academy will also offer some tours and activities that you might want to take advantage of.

Remember to have realistic expectations for the time you will spend together. Keep in mind that weekend will be the mids' first chance to get out of Bancroft Hall since I-Day. Most mids will be dying to get to a room—quickly—where they can get out of their uniform and "crash" for a few hours. Mostly they will want lots of junk food, a long shower, some sleep, and a chance to watch anything on television. It would definitely be an exceptional mid who would want to do much sightseeing.

Will they want to talk about everything that has been happening to them? Maybe. If so, some of what they say will sound like a foreign language, with terms and acronyms you have never heard before. Be ready to lend an ear and offer support and perspective. For some, the experience may be more than they can put into words, or they may want to forget about plebe life completely. Let them choose.

Be ready to see some dramatic changes in your son or daughter, say the parents. Here are some of their comments.

A father from Oregon: "Be prepared for an emotionally mummified kid. They all look the same. They are almost catatonic. She sat at attention in the chair when we got into the motel. It took her awhile to unwind. Later she relaxed and took us sailing and she was more normal."

A mother from Pennsylvania: "When you see him, he is no longer your little boy—they have matured a lot. We teased him about one thing. He was always walking ahead of us and looking at his watch worrying about being on time—that was a big change."

A father from Florida: "We picked him up at Wendy's and while he was in the back seat on our way to Burger King [where he wanted to go], he went to sleep while we were talking to him."

A single mother from Arkansas: "I thought he looked great—he was really handsome even though he had lost about 30 pounds. He was really proud of making it through Plebe Summer and to see him there getting along okay made everything right. But all he wanted at first was to go to the room and crash; then he wanted pizza; then he slept some more. I just sat and watched him sleep. Later we walked around the school; then we sat by the water and talked for a long time."

For some, the experience may be more than they can put into words.

Another father from New York: "We took her directly to the motel and had planned on going to the pool, then to dinner. But she sat on the bed and talked for three solid hours. I regret now not having a tape recorder because she told of experiences that she will never tell in that way again. I recommend that parents take one for that first long conversation. To see her so charged up was the high point of the visit."

A father from Minnesota: "They want to talk, to tell you everything and the worst thing parents can do is yawn when the kid is excited and telling all those things. Don't be judgmental and say that it is immature or silly. Just sit and listen."

A mother from Arkansas: "Expect a new son or daughter because they are different. They are more respectful of their parents and of each other, and all the parents we spoke with commented on how much the kids had matured. One woman said they had taught her son more in five weeks than she and her husband had in eighteen years. Unlike most, however, our son did not look haggard and tired. But I can't forget that look on his face in that crowd of a thousand mids. He had a stern look but a big grin was about to bust out and you could tell his eyes were on nobody but us. He hugged us and talked—we had never been greeted like that before—that's why it stands out in my mind so much."

One controversial issue among parents is whether or not girlfriends and boyfriends should go along on Parents' Weekend. Here are some sample comments:

A mother from Georgia: "The girlfriend went with us and it was a bad experience. We strongly recommend that you leave the girlfriend home—although it might work out with the right kind of girl. Our son was going with an immature girl. And there he was, emotionally drained from six weeks of constant trauma and he had to divide his time between us. It was not a relaxing weekend and it should have been. Let the girl go later for a weekend dance or a football game. Of course, now they have broken up."

A mother from Minnesota: "We thought the girlfriend did him a lot of good—that it helped his morale a lot. We look at her as a good friend of the family and we didn't feel torn. We knew the girl pretty well. Our family has always been very open with comments and feelings and we just talked about everything all the time as though she was a daughter and we didn't feel that she was an imposition."

The mids call it Black Sunday because the first classmen are just waiting for them.

A mother from Virginia: "I am biased because I was the girlfriend when my husband was a plebe at the Academy. Obviously it worked out okay! I still treasure the picture his parents took of the two of us on the Capitol steps."

A mother from Illinois and co-president of a parents' club: "Our daughter's boyfriend went along and we now advise parents not to let this happen. The young man wanted her to spend her free time with him rather than us. That created problems between the two of them as well as with us. Fortunately that relationship was over by Thanksgiving."

One of the hardest things during Parents' Weekend is saying goodbye, especially after the mids tell their parents what they can expect when they return to Bancroft Hall Sunday night. The mids call it Black Sunday because the first classmen are just waiting for them. As the mids gather to say goodbye, the first classmen are hanging out the windows with Christmas music playing loudly on their stereos, saying that you are not going to be seeing mommy and daddy until Christmas. And when the plebes return to their rooms, they are subjected to all kinds of harassment just to get them back into the groove of Plebe Summer. As an example, one mid told how his room had been trashed and how, with the lights out, he and his roommates had to put it back in order.

Try to be positive as you say goodbye.
USNA PHOTO LAB

So, make your goodbyes short, said many parents. And try to be good actors. Do not let your emotions run over, because the mids have some very difficult hours ahead of them. They do not need the haunting images of mom and dad or girlfriends crying, say the parents. What they need is to be left with strong, positive feelings of support, and a conviction that the parents will continue to support them in the future. After all, they have only gone through about five and one-half weeks of the plebe indoctrination system. They still have one very long, difficult plebe year ahead of them.

A parents' club president from Massachusetts cautioned, "Also be sensitive to the mids' time constraints. Remember, 900 mids are trying to get back to Bancroft Hall for the same curfew. And, if they are late, they can't say to their company officer, 'I'm sorry, my mother just wanted to go into one more shop.' You have to respect their time schedule. Allow adequate time to get back to the yard and plan for traffic jams! If your mid is at Gate One five minutes before the curfew, he is going to have trouble getting to Bancroft Hall on time."

One final bit of advice regarding Parents' Weekend comes from an Arkansas mother. She said, "Don't forget about the siblings. It's so easy to get caught up in talking about the midshipman all the time, especially when everybody in the town is calling and asking about him. It's real easy for the brothers and sisters at home to feel that they have become second-class citizens. Try to give them attention, too, and involve them in the planning for parents' weekend if they're going. They have to feel that they're important, too."

THE LONG PLEBE YEAR

Once Plebe Summer is over and the academic year begins, the plebe experience changes significantly. During Plebe Summer, plebes work as part of a team every minute; they are told what to do and when to do it. They are pushed hard, but they have very few decisions to make.

Once the academic year starts, they must learn to manage their time. Typically, the plebe is very bright and was able to get excellent grades in high school just by sitting in classes and listening. Most have never been challenged, and therefore they do not know how to study. They try, of course. But they are loaded down with far more academic work than they can accomplish with their old, inefficient study habits.

Also, they are pressured by upperclassmen to learn a lot of military information called "rates." Assignments pile up and many are left undone. Then the plebe gets behind and the situation deteriorates. Plebes who carried a near 4.0 grade point average in high school find themselves with an unsatisfactory 1.72 at midterm and, perhaps meeting an academic board that decides whether to keep them or send them home.

One word of assurance: nearly 80 percent of entering plebes will make it through all four years and graduate. However, very few will get through without some serious struggles. Nearly every plebe will experience failure and question their ability to survive the year at some point. Parents are the one who will hear these doubts, and sense the frustration and unhappiness their superstar child is wrestling with. Almost every parent who was interviewed said that new parents need more help with downer telephone calls than anything else. The following comments present a broad sampling of that advice.

> *Nearly every plebe will experience failure and question their ability to survive the year at some point.*

A father from Georgia: "In our parents' club we always ask parents from each class to talk to the new parents and the subject always gets around to the downer phone calls. The thing we always stress is this: Those young men and women are a bit selfish and their world has turned upside down. They will make calls home and it will put great demands upon your time and emotions. They will call one Sunday and be at the bottom of the pit. The next Sunday they call and they are up and okay, yet the parents will worry all week. The new parent must realize that their [the mid's] whole temperament can change in 30 seconds—that's just part of it. If possible, parents should share those experiences and laugh about them. We had one mother call us—she was upset because her son had chosen to go there and then he calls up and complains all the time. We explained that he needs someone to dump on—that he is being yelled at by everybody and can't do anything right because that's the system. We explained that there's no way to change any of that, so the mid needs someone to talk to."

A father from Oregon: "When they call and start hinting around about quitting, it's common for parents to start worrying. They have to realize that such thoughts are normal—there's hardly anyone who doesn't think about quitting any college. But what's important is for the mid to know he has your support if he does quit—that it's not a social stigma. The Naval Academy is not for everybody. Of course, it's important not to quit on a whim."

A mother from California with one Academy graduate and another mid there now: "They need encouragement to stick it out when they call and are down. You've got to say, 'You've made it this far—there's only a couple of weeks to this or that—there's only a couple of weeks to the Army-Navy game or a couple of weeks till Christmas. It is normal that they want to quit."

The biggest asset you bring as a parent is perspective. Feel free to share it.

A mother from Florida: "Deep down you may feel that it is all coming to an end [the daughter went before several academic boards] but when you speak to them, you make every thing positive. You emphasize positive thinking again and again. I remember finding this wonderful article on personal fortitude by a Vietnam POW and I sent that to her. You can't let your barriers down when they call—they don't call for you to tell them negative things. She knew I was feeling it but I couldn't tell her how much. When you hang up, then you cry. You have to be a good actress. The happiest day of my life was when I saw her graduate and I said, 'Thank you, God!'"

They're going to find they'll associate with some of the best, most motivated people in the world.

Said another parent, who is also a graduate, "Encourage them to doing a full year plus the summer [after plebe year] and see what it's really about. The Academy is not the Navy. Summer in the fleet is the spark that will light their fire. They have to see officers and sailors and talk to them and find out what they do. They're going to find they'll associate with some of the best, most motivated people in the world. They should go in with mindset that no matter what, they're not going to stay for less than a full year."

You also have to know them well enough to realize that the Academy really is not the right place for them. They need more support at this time than any other. A father who is also a graduate: "You have to encourage them but you should also know your child well enough to listen. You have to ask them [when they start talking about quitting] what plans they have and what alternatives they are thinking about. But you have to be very careful to make sure what a parent considers encouragement is not strong encouragement. You owe it to them to continue to encourage them, but if they make up their mind to leave, you also owe it to them to encourage them at that. Just make sure that they are doing it for a good reason."

The next question is, what should a parent do if they believe their mid is becoming severely depressed? The first question to ask the mid is: Have you talked with anyone there at the Academy about your problem? If the mid answers in the affirmative, there is less reason to worry. At least the mid is not bottling up his problems, which is a harbinger of potential trouble.

If the mid has not spoken to anyone about his problem, then several courses of action have been recommended. One is to get on the phone with the Company Officer and discuss your concerns. Many of them are sensitive to the kinds of problems the mids encounter because they are graduates themselves. Another is to contact the Midshipman Counseling Center. The third course of action is to phone one of the chaplains. Just call the Academy switchboard (410-293-1000).

What if there is an apparent real emergency that has to be handled immediately and it is after hours? The advice from the Academy is to tell the switchboard operator that you have a possible emergency and that you must speak to the Officer of the Watch.

There is also the possibility that a mid will get injured or become ill and be placed in a hospital. If this happens, parents are sometimes frustrated when trying to get information. If this should happen to your mid, call the Company Officer first and get the name of the mid's attending physician and the number where he or she can be reached. If the Company Officer does not have that information, have the switchboard operator connect you with the Branch Medical Clinic in Bancroft Hall and they should be able to tell you what you need to know. If the preceding steps fail, then speak with one of the chaplains who will be certain to help you.

Keep the letters coming.
Keep the packages coming.
Enlist the help of family
friends and relatives...

Most plebes will not spend the majority of the year feeling down or needing professional help. But they all need support. The same support systems that got them through Plebe Summer will help them through the year. Keep the letters coming. Keep the packages coming. Enlist the help of family friends and relatives to make sure their mailbox does not become a nest of cobwebs. Send pictures, the local paper, anything to distract your plebe from Academy life for a moment and bring a smile.

What about e-mail? Here is the story on e-mail. The mids all expect to get dozens and sometimes hundreds of e-mail communications every day. Many are "in-house" memos from professors, announcements of Academy activities, etc. But many of them are from friends in the Brigade—friends made during Plebe Summer but who are now dispersed throughout the huge Bancroft Hall. And, yes, there are also many e-mail letters from parents, brothers and sisters, and high school friends who are in other colleges. So e-mail is an important part of the mids' life, and, in terms of advice for parents, the author makes a strong recommendation that you stay in contact by e-mail.

However, after speaking with about 200 mids—mostly plebes in the late part of their year—their overwhelming advice was to tell parents not to forget about regular mail! They were adamant about this advice. They feel strongly that e-mail is sort of a "quick and dirty" way to communicate, while regular mail takes more time and effort. The plebes emphasized that the extra time and effort means a lot to them—that it is a way parents can demonstrate that they really care.

Many mids find the volume of e-mail they receive a distraction from their studies and other duties. They might not respond to your e-mails, leaving you wondering what is going on. Said one, "With my parents, I said I'm not going to really respond to you via e-mail. I'm going to call you on a regular basis. I will read your e-mails but I'm not going to respond to them." If your son or daughter decides to handle e-mails this way, do not be hurt. Respect their maturity in coming up with a system that works for them.

And what about cell phones? Most midshipmen have one. Parents benefit from this, because the midshipmen can call home whenever they find a spare moment. However, do not expect them to answer voice mail or text messages all of the time. Most of them will leave their phones in their rooms, turned off, most of the time. They are busy with other things. Many midshipmen set a regular time to call home, such as Sunday afternoons.

If you do not want to buy a regular cell phone and full service, it is recommended that you buy your son or daughter a pre-paid cell phone. These are fairly inexpensive and provide a precious and easy link to home.

OTHER ADVICE

Many parents warmly praised the Naval Academy Plebe Sponsor Program. This is a program where families from the Annapolis area "adopt" one or more plebes and bring them to their homes on weekends when the plebes are free. The idea is to give the plebes a "home away from home"— a place where they can relax and get away from all the pressure. Often the sponsor relationship continues after the plebe year and in some cases the mid-sponsor relationship becomes a lifelong friendship. (A parent in Ohio told of their son's sponsor who traveled to Ohio for his wedding!)

What parents should realize about the sponsor program is that it is too valuable not to be used by a plebe. In some cases, the first visit does not go well and the plebe decides just to stay in Bancroft Hall. Encourage your plebe not to do that. Encourage your plebe to contact the Plebe Sponsor Program Coordinator and ask for another sponsor. An alternative, which many plebes stumble into, is to tag along with a roommate who has a compatible sponsor. Just remember, your plebe needs to get away once in awhile and a good sponsor can make life at the Academy much more bearable.

Midshipman support is a very important role for parents. But that support should also be broadened, where possible, to mids other than the son or daughter. Several parents mentioned the son or daughter's roommates and how much they appreciate a funny card now and then or a little note wishing them well on a chemistry test.

Also, if you live reasonably close to the Academy, you might want to invite one of your son or daughter's friends who can't get home for Thanksgiving to your own home. Parents who have done that highly recommend it to others.

Also, do not forget your son or daughter's classmates when you visit the Academy. They like to get away and greatly appreciate a chance to be with another family. They also appreciate the more elemental things, such as what was described by a Texas father who had a son and daughter there:

"I was back for a visit and I was taken to my son's room where I greeted him with a big hug. His roommate, about six-five and a basketball player, looked down at me like I was a midget and asked sheepishly, 'Can I have a hug, too, sir?' All he wanted was a touch of family. About the same thing happened one time when I greeted my daughter with a hug. The girl with her handed her books to my daughter and, for reasons I can't go into now, the hug I gave her might have been a turning point for that kid. So my advice is just don't hug your kid; hug them all!"

Another issue is whether plebes need extra spending money. Plebes will receive about $100 per month to take care of personal supplies. Some parents supplement this pay. Others feel that is not necessary. Said one, "My daughter had enough money left over from summer jobs. They have few needs that aren't covered, maybe an occasional movie on weekends. Plebe year, they shouldn't need more except at holidays. We did give her a credit card for emergencies, so if she got left by a bus she'd have the ability to get somewhere." They will probably also need help funding plane tickets or other transportation home over the holidays.

A FINAL WORD OF ADVICE FROM THE AUTHOR

I still remember something my father said many years ago, at the celebration banquet the night before my own graduation ceremony from the Air Force Academy: "I want you to know, these last four years were a lot harder on your mother than they were on you!" I never knew she had worried about me so much, because (thank goodness) she never told me.

Now, as a sponsor of several Air Force cadets, I find myself in the role of counselor to worried parents. Here is a condensed version of what I tell them:

They will be fine. They have what it takes to get through. They may not always have a lot of fun, and they will face some struggles and challenges. Sometimes you will feel their pain when they call home. Nonetheless, the same Academy system that pushes them hard and sometimes makes them miserable will also take very good care of them. They will be better and stronger in the end, and they will be glad they stuck it out.

If your son or daughter chooses to go to the Naval Academy and receives an appointment, be confident in the values and abilities you sent them off with.

Tell them often that they are great kids—they need to hear that during the plebe year. And rest assured that they are becoming part of a long and proud tradition of Naval Academy graduates who have served their country with honor and excelled in life.

Best Wishes and Good Luck,
SCR

ACKNOWLEDGMENTS

My thanks must begin and end with the wise and talented Bill Smallwood, whose passion for helping young men and women find their path to success guides everything in this book. His vision, thorough research, and straightforward writing style are evident in the earlier editions of this book. If I have succeeded in this third edition, it is only because I have successfully copied his approach.

Hundreds of other people helped with this and previous editions of this book, and I cannot name them all. But to all the administrators, professors, congressional staffers, parents, and blue and gold officers, thank you for your time and insights.

Special thanks are due to Judy Campbell and the Naval Academy Public Affairs Office for coordinating interviews, answering questions, and providing other resources. They have been very supportive of this project and our efforts at getting the story straight.

The intercollegiate chapter is new to this edition. Thanks to David Davis from the Athletic Association for his insights and help in connecting with graduate athletes.

Thanks also to Commander Tom Schwarz from the Officer Development Division, Lieutenant Commander Chip Crane from the Writing Center, Dr. Eric Bowman from the Academic Center, and Lieutenant Schuyler Morse and Lieutenant John Tasch from Admissions. Thanks to Bobbi Collins from the Alumni Association for helping me contact graduates.

I also want to thank the many midshipmen and graduates who shared their stories—their pain and struggles as well as their successes and joys. Though I cannot list all of you by name, I thank you for sharing your experiences.

I must end by repeating my thanks to Bill Smallwood and also his wife Patricia, for your mentorship and friendship, and for trusting me to carry on your work.

INDEX

<u>*To Order Additional Copies:*</u>

Visit **www.navyonline.com**
Also available from Amazon.com

<u>*Also Available from Silver Horn Books:*</u>

The Air Force Academy Candidate Book **$18.95**
Visit www.goairforcefalcons.com
or Amazon.com

The West Point Candidate Book **$18.95**
Available from Amazon.com